appartient à

Rendu à Lia. ~1/1/2024.

Peter

Colonel Strutt's Daring Royal Mission

For Alan – best of husbands with all my love.

Colonel Strutt's Daring Royal Mission

The Secret British Rescue of the Habsburg Family, 1919

The full story of the audacious rescue of the Imperial Habsburg family in April 1919, based on the diary – "Three Months of 1919" written by Lieutenant Colonel Edward Lisle Strutt CBE, DSO. Royal Scots Fusiliers, Croix de Guerre with four Palms, Chevalier and Officer of the Legion of Honour, Chevalier of the Order of St Leopold, Belgian Croix de Guerre and Palm, Order of the Star of Romania.

Diana Tritton

PEN & SWORD
HISTORY

First published in Great Britain in 2023 by
Pen & Sword History
An imprint of
Pen & Sword Books Ltd
Yorkshire – Philadelphia

ISBN 978 1 39906 042 4

A CIP catalogue record for this book is
available from the British Library.

Typeset by Mac Style
Printed and bound in the UK by CPI Group (UK) Ltd,
Croydon, CR0 4YY.

Pen & Sword Books Limited incorporates the imprints of Atlas,
Archaeology, Aviation, Discovery, Family History, Fiction, History,
Maritime, Military, Military Classics, Politics, Select, Transport,
True Crime, Air World, Frontline Publishing, Leo Cooper, Remember
When, Seaforth Publishing, The Praetorian Press, Wharncliffe
Local History, Wharncliffe Transport, Wharncliffe True Crime
and White Owl.

For a complete list of Pen & Sword titles please contact

PEN & SWORD BOOKS LIMITED
47 Church Street, Barnsley, South Yorkshire, S70 2AS, England
E-mail: enquiries@pen-and-sword.co.uk
Website: www.pen-and-sword.co.uk

Or

PEN AND SWORD BOOKS
1950 Lawrence Rd, Havertown, PA 19083, USA
E-mail: Uspen-and-sword@casematepublishers.com
Website: www.penandswordbooks.com

Contents

Introduction

The First World War left large parts of Europe in ruins. Millions of people were displaced, millions died and four Empires collapsed – the Ottoman, Russian, German and Austro-Hungarian. Worse, a red tide of Communism was now seeping its way through Eastern Europe and the Spanish Influenza was about to strike millions more. For many thousands all was lost, but for one lucky Imperial couple help was at hand from an unexpected quarter.

This is the story of how King George V of England felt impelled to rescue the Imperial Habsburg Family – whom he hardly knew, whom he had been fighting for four years and to whom he was in no way related. At the time, the British public's hatred of all things German, which included Austria-Hungary, was virulent. It was politically impossible for the King to be seen overtly helping his former adversary; his own position could have been imperilled. Yet to his great credit he did dare to extend his hand to them, but of course in deepest secrecy.

The man chosen for the job was Lieutenant Colonel Edward Lisle Strutt, who had spent the last three years at Salonika, Greece on the Eastern Front. His official role there was that of senior liaison officer between the British and French Macedonian commanders, but this understates what his job actually entailed.

The Eastern Front, unlike its better known counterpart, was not bogged down in the horrors of the trenches. It was not static. It ranged over thousands of miles from the Black Sea to the Baltic; five separate theatres of operation lined the route, and many nations were involved in the struggle. I have tried to give the flavour of what the Allied troops were up against fighting in a place totally unsuited to modern warfare. In Macedonia, for instance, there were few wells, few roads, insufficient forage and food, no transport to speak of, no survey maps. Everything had to be imported for the army by British warships dodging German U-boats in the eastern Mediterranean. It was expensive and brutal.

From his diary and the few records of his movements during the war which have survived, it appears that Colonel Strutt had proved himself a consummate strategist during the eighteen months he worked at MI3 (Intelligence) in London early in the war. He was clever, resourceful and above all prescient. His forte was a talent to get to the heart of a problem quickly and solve it. His gift for languages also made him an important liaison between commanders of disparate national armies. He was sent to Salonika in 1916 to do his best to bang heads together and he did not disappoint.

In January 1919, when David Lloyd George, the Prime Minister, was charged by his King to find the ideal man to aid the Habsburg, it was remembered that amongst Strutt's other sterling qualities, he was well travelled, cultured and socially adept. The fact that he was also a Roman Catholic probably cemented the Prime Minister's decision to choose him for the very delicate job of extracting the Catholic Habsburg from Austria if it came to it. If it all went wrong, on the other hand, they were confident Strutt would know how to keep the British government out of it. They would, naturally, have to deny everything.

This is also a story of loss and redemption, of how a man found peace after staggering victorious from history's most calamitous war only to find that in the winning he had lost most of that which he had held dear. He wasn't alone in his suffering by any means, but his hidden sensitivity to injustice and cruelty made the ruination of his world hurt all the more.

Strutt's type of man is rare nowadays, which is why this story might seem remote to modern readers who are unfamiliar with the mindset of the British people before the First World War. For more than a century, the British Empire had imbued the British people with the conviction that they were the pre-eminent race on the planet, and they expected to be treated as such. Britannia ruled a third of the world and as far as they were concerned, it was not by accident. They had reached this eminence by force of arms and intellect, and they took enormous pride in it. Strutt's confidence was rooted in this conviction. He was a Victorian boots and spurs.

In his day, an officer in a top regiment like the Guards, the Blues and Royals, the Scots Greys or the Scots Royal Fusiliers was considered to be first and foremost a gentleman whose honour was unquestioned; like medieval knights of old, the upper classes led in war and other ranks loyally supported them. Thus, a British army officer was considered brave, resourceful and expected to be obeyed. Not all of them lived up to this ideal, of course, but that was the standard. Indeed, few men had Strutt's multi-faceted strength of character, but they aspired to it.

Appreciations

My thanks go to my wonderful husband, Alan, for his continuing encouragement without which I would never have finished this book. I must also thank Cornerstones for helping me to bring the story together and finally, special thanks go to Lieutenant General Sir Anthony Denison-Smith for his invaluable advice and for his patience in answering my endless questions about military matters. All mistakes are mine.

Lt Colonel Edward Lisle Strutt.

HOUSE OF HABSBURG-LORRAINE

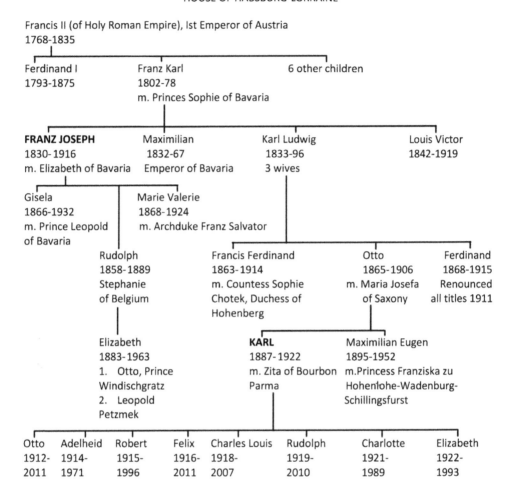

Francis II (of Holy Roman Empire), Ist Emperor of Austria
1768-1835

Ferdinand I
1793-1875

Franz Karl
1802-78
m. Princes Sophie of Bavaria

6 other children

FRANZ JOSEPH
1830-1916
m. Elizabeth of Bavaria

Maximilian
1832-67
Emperor of Bavaria

Karl Ludwig
1833-96
3 wives

Louis Victor
1842-1919

Gisela
1866-1932
m. Prince Leopold
of Bavaria

Marie Valerie
1868-1924
m. Archduke Franz Salvator

Rudolph
1858-1889
Stephanie
of Belgium

Francis Ferdinand
1863-1914
m. Countess Sophie
Chotek, Duchess of
Hohenberg

Otto
1865-1906
m. Maria Josefa
of Saxony

Ferdinand
1868-1915
Renounced
all titles 1911

Elizabeth
1883-1963
1.   Otto, Prince
Windischgratz
2.   Leopold
Petzmek

KARL
1887-1922
m. Zita of Bourbon
Parma

Maximilian Eugen
1895-1952
m.Princess Franziska zu
Hohenlohe-Wadenburg-
Schillingsfurst

Otto	Adelheid	Robert	Felix	Charles Louis	Rudolph	Charlotte	Elizabeth
1912-	1914-	1915-	1916-	1918-	1919-	1921-	1922-
2011	1971	1996	2011	2007	2010	1989	1993

STRUTT FAMILY TREE

<u>Jedediah Strutt</u> – 1726-1797
Derbyshire hosier and cotton spinner. Inventor and later partner of Richard Arkwright who is
credited with being the "father of the modern industrial factory system."

<u>William Strutt</u> 1756-1830
Civil engineer, architect and mill owner

<u>Edward Strutt</u> 1801-80
cr. Baron Belper 1856
Politician, industrialist. Built Kingston Hall, Notts.

<u>William</u>	<u>Henry</u>	<u>Arthur</u>
1838-56	1840-1914	1842-77
	2nd Baron	m. 1873 Alice
	MP	Phillipps de Lisle*
	Capt. of HM's Corps of Gentlemen at Arms 1895-1906	
	Married 1874 Lady Margaret Coke, dau. Of Earl of Leic.	

<u>William</u>	<u>Reginald</u>	<u>Algernon Henry</u>	**Edward Lisle**
1875-98	1881-88	1883-1956	1874-1948
		3rd Baron, a soldier	m. Florence Hollond
			dau. of John Hollond
			of Wonham, Devon
			&
			Laura May
			1875-1909
			m. 1903 Capt. Ed.
			Charlton RN. 3 dau.

1st wife Hon. Eva Bruce   2nd wife Angela Tollemache
div. 1922

<u>Alex. Ronald George</u>	<u>Michael</u>	<u>Lavinia</u>	<u>Peter</u>	<u>Desmond Rupert</u>
1912-99	1914-1942	1916-95	1924-2007	1926-93
4th Baron		m. 16th		
		Duke		
		of Norfolk		

*Daughter of Ambrose Lisle March Phillipps de Lisle 1809-1878, famously influential English Catholic
convert. "One of the wealthiest commoners in England". Lived at Grace Dieu Manor, Leics. on the site
of an Augustine Priory. His goal was the reunification of the Catholic and Protestant wings of the
Christian church. When Alice was widowed after less than five years of marriage, she divided her time
between her own family of ten siblings centred in Leicestershire and the Belper estate in
Nottinghamshire. She never married again.

Chapter One

February 5, 1919
Salonika

This was the end at last. The five remaining officers stood wearily on the stony bluff overlooking the port of Salonika. High above them a flight of sea gulls circled the beach, their excited shrieks filling the cold air. It was 3 o'clock on a stormy afternoon. Rain would come soon. The men were watching the last of the horses being loaded on to the last of the frigates. In the far distance, HMS Resolute was steaming towards the horizon through the white-whipped sea. The crossing to Crete would be rough.

On the beach directly below them for half a mile in each direction, lay a vast wreckage of tin supply boxes all tumbled together with abandoned army vehicles. Crowds of men and women, dressed in rags were picking over them. The sea gulls, dive-bombing, were giving them competition.

The history books say that the First World War, the Great War, ended officially on 11 November 1918, but that wasn't really so. There were the residual hold-outs to contend with and the clean up to oversee. You cannot unwind everything it takes to fight a war immediately, especially in a place like Macedonia with no resources of its own. 'Might as well fight on the Moon', the sceptics had shouted in Whitehall when it was first bruited in the spring of 1915. The new theatre of war in Macedonia had cost the Allies eye-watering sums, but it was a price worth paying if it meant that a quantity of German divisions would be tied to the Eastern Front. No one regretted it. They just hated it.

The officers left behind to supervise the pull-out had been working solidly for nearly three months and today really was the finish. Lt Colonel Edward Lisle Strutt, Royal Scots Fusiliers, adjusted his muffler and looked at his watch. Yes, he thought, looking at his French comrades who were silently pondering the view with their own reflections, it's a sight we will never forget. 'Let's get to the train,' he called brusquely. 'We're done here.'

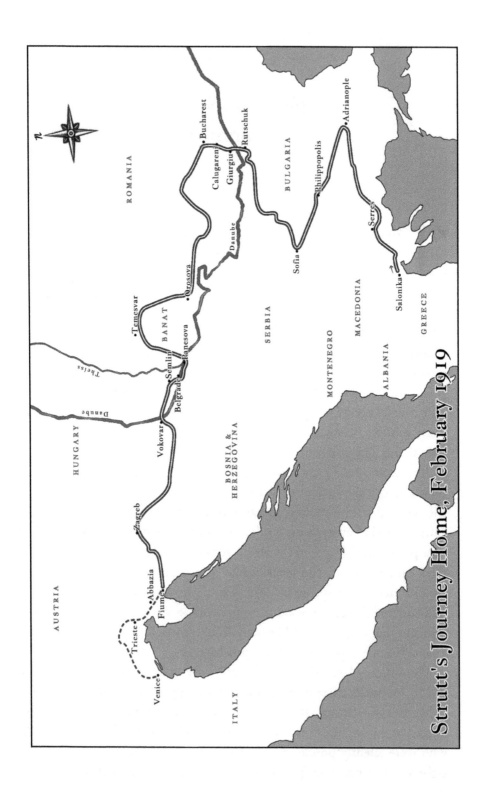

Strutt's Journey Home, February 1919

At the station, which had been hastily rebuilt and extended three years ago, a special train with four carriages and a few loaded flats sat steaming as it waited. For once they had asked for accommodation on an undamaged train and got it. Vadrot at work again, he supposed. What a blessing the man was to have around; such a pity he was such a cynical bastard.

First to climb on board was General Paul-Prosper Henrys KCB, Commander of the French Army of the Orient formed in Macedonia during the last few years. He was fifty-six years old, of average height, grey hair and boasted a fulsome moustache of which he was very fond. Strutt considered him a first class leader of men with very little 'side'. In other words, he did not stand on ceremony. In addition, he didn't take too much offense at the laughter that occurred behind his back whenever he combed his moustache, which was frequently. Strutt knew Henrys' affability concealed a very clever brain which he respected. He might be informal amongst friends, but it was not wise to cross him.

With him were his ADC's Captain Vadrot and Lieutenant Prince Paul Murat. Colonel du Tilly, a liaison officer, accompanied them. Strutt entered last. They had reserved the car for themselves and were delighted to find the saloon comfortably appointed. It was mid-afternoon.

General Henrys seated himself heavily and inspected the accommodation. It was superb, he must remember to award Vadrot another medal for finding it. The saloon was positively pre-war with polished wooden panelling, comfortable blue plush easy chairs, a sofa and even a games table with matching upright chairs. He lifted an eyebrow at Vadrot in question. Vadrot, preening, swore the Bulgarians stole it from the Hungarians and he had been just lucky to find it.

Henrys immediately translated this information in his head. Vadrot had stolen the train. This was a disgrace, but when all things were considered, he mused, was it stealing to rob a thief? He smiled benevolently at Vadrot. Strutt watched this interplay with amusement and laughed out loud when Vadrot winked at him and whispered, 'the trick was to keep it hidden until we needed it!'

Vadrot was Henrys' quartermaster, friend, valet, and spy when required. He was tall and rather swarthy which indicated an Algerian mother. Strutt thought he looked a bit sinister, but the women seemed to like his crocodile smile and seductive eyes. They were always watching him when he walked by in the villages.

Lieutenant Murat, not heeding the conversation, threw himself into a chair still bragging again about the last minute sale of the mules. The Greeks actually thought that if they waited long enough, the Army would just leave them behind – for free, all two hundred of them, which the French had brought in from North Africa at great expense. Murat was delighted he had outsmarted them. He was a small, slender young man with large dark eyes and a shock of black hair which he tried to keep down with pomade, to no avail. A cowlick stood up like a sail. It was full of energy like himself. His uniform was dusty from the animal pens and his long leather boots needed a good clean. He might lack the elegance of his ancestor, Prince Paul Murat, Napoleon's brother-in-law, but he made up for it by being an extremely efficient administrator.

Strutt told him he was too hard. The Greeks wanted the mules to eat. Murat looked at him in disgust. Of course, he knew that, but first they wanted the mules to carry away the discarded materiel on the beach which was worth another fortune. Strutt asked him how he managed to get them to pay for the mules. Murat's face took on a canny look. He threatened to shoot them all, of course. Strutt's slight amusement ended. The Greek people were starving. He knew this. His mind pictured them having to butcher the helpless mules all in one go and the cloud of depression he'd been fighting all day descended. The French did not share the British sentimentality towards animals.

Captain Vadrot had stowed his gear in his compartment and was back to do the same for Henrys and his baggage. They could all do with a rest and a wash before dinner. He did not want to hear, smell or pull a mule out of the mud again ever. He looked around. Where was the staff he ordered?

Just then, Du Tilly rejoined them after arranging his kit to his satisfaction. His little round head beamed with smiles as he shut the door to the bedroom corridor. There was something child-like about this thirty-five year-old liaison officer, but he carried messages well enough. Looking at his rather silly face, Strutt could not conceive how the French had made him a colonel.

Du Tilly had the pleasure of assuring them all that a proper kitchen wagon had been attached to the train along with a cook and a few staff. Vadrot was relieved. There was also sufficient wine on board. He had made sure the last of Henrys' hoard would accompany them on the journey. They all turned and bowed to the General who waved his hand in a princely manner as he followed Vadrot out of the saloon.

Now, confident that the next four to five days would be as comfortable as possible, Strutt left them arguing and went to his own quarters as the train departed the station. They were on their way to Bucharest where Henrys had been ordered to report. Then they would spend some days in Belgrade followed by Zagreb and then Venice where they would all go their separate ways.

Strutt might have gone home separately, but not any faster. The trains were all down to the east and all British shipping had retreated from Greece. He might as well accompany Henrys and the others as far as Venice. His last task before he could go home was to report his intelligence findings to Constantinople, where his supreme commander, General Sir Tom Bridges was now stationed.

The war might be over, but intelligence gathering was still vitally important particularly in Eastern Europe. Nobody trusted the Germans or their allies. It was possible they could rise again if the conditions were right and the Treaty terms were too harsh. Then there was the danger of Communism. How bad was it? This long journey should give him a good understanding of public opinion on the ground. His superiors didn't think it wise for the Allies to drop their guard yet awhile.

Sitting on the bed, Strutt felt grubby and out of sorts. This should be a happy day, but somehow he felt empty. He had longed to leave the pest hole of Salonika, but it was a familiar pest hole. He was almost frightened to see what the war had done to Central Europe in the last two years. The Austro-Hungarian Empire had been his stamping ground long before the war. He'd been at school there for a time and made many friends. After he joined the army, he still went there to ski and shoot. It had all been such fun. He had loved it there.

His bones, however, had been telling him for months that the glittering world of pre-war Europe was utterly destroyed and wouldn't come again. Only the thought of home and Florrie, his wife, kept him going. Was the effort of survival going to be worth the effort, he wondered? That was the big question. He was so very tired. Mercifully, there was a hot shower in the cubicle next to his compartment and after that he lay down for a nap. The noise of the train and the slight vibration soothed him and he slept.

Strutt had been assigned by General Bridges, then the Commander of the British Salonika Force, to take over as the top Liaison Officer between the French General Henrys and the British General Milne, but he had spent more time recently with the former. Milne, the Commander of the British Macedonian Front based at Salonika had gone home early to be made a Field Marshal.

As it happened, there had been as much work at the end of the war as at the beginning, so he and his French colleagues had been forced to stay behind to supervise it. First, all the portable armaments, food, fodder, horses and their keepers had to be gathered for transport home. This took weeks. Then the ships had to be organised to take the troops and everything else in proper sequence. It took forever. Not only his language skills were required, but in the end his organisational expertise as well. Too many officers had been killed or wounded. There was no one else.

Their train would stop first at Adrianople on the Turkish border. After that, there would be many stops on the way to Sofia. From there they would leave the train at Rustchuk on the Danube where they would cross to make their way to Bucharest. He needn't worry about what would happen after that. They would be informed.

Strutt slept for three hours under warm blankets and felt better. Now it was time for a drink and some food. He found Henrys and Vadrot in the saloon car enjoying both. They too were in better form after a good rest and greeted him cordially. Knowing Strutt's interest in railways and bridges, Henrys pointed to the window. The Demir Hasaar bridge was just coming into view. Built not so long ago over the Struma River in northern Greece, it was a fine piece of engineering. Strutt admired the view up the snowy Rupel Gorge. It was magnificent and so was Mount Rhodope towering over it in the background. He then casually informed them the speed should increase soon.

Henrys laughed. How was it that he was so unbelievably knowledgeable about trains and timetables? Did they teach that in British schools? Did students have to chant out train tables the same way as they did their mathematical times tables? Did the British army consider train tables an essential tool of war? If so, it was damn clever. The train was now running very slowly over the Struma Flats on an entirely reconstructed line to Seres at which point the speed did improve as Strutt said it would.

Strutt always liked the affable Henrys. He had a sense of humour and liked to tease. He explained that while working at Military Intelligence in London earlier in the war, he came to realise that he who understood European time tables and the terrain, held a weapon in his hands. Henrys quickly covered his ears and told him to stop. He accepted Strutt was undoubtedly right, but the war was over and he didn't have to bother with all that again, thank God. He now wanted his dinner and suggested they all played bridge afterwards.

And so, time passed, the comrades rose mid-morning, breakfasted, and went out for walks and fresh air whenever the train stopped for any length of time. Like soldiers everywhere, they periodically thrashed out their memories of previous fighting, particularly the last great battle in September 1918 at Dobro Pole in Bulgaria which ended the war on the Eastern Front.

That had been a desperate time quite outside anyone's experience. Both sides were exhausted after four years of conflict; thousands of troops had died of malaria, dysentery or had just plain deserted. Food was scare. All kinds of promises of support were made by various Allies, but in the end the force facing the Central Powers was not a large one. Their ally, the Russians had retreated from the war after the Treaty of Brest-Litovsk[1] in March and were busy with a civil war of their own.

So on the day, the Allied forces consisted of the last remnants of the Greek Army including a Cretan division and a Greek Archipelago division. The French Army of the Orient was also there. It included some French, Italian and French/African Colonial brigades. Also present was the last of the Serbian Army. The British Salonika Force and the British 27th infantry division had been thrown in as well to give added strength.

On the other side, fielding a smaller force, were the Central Powers, consisting of a Bulgarian division and a few German brigades. The Bulgarians were outnumbered, but they had the advantage of being on home ground. Both sides were at the last ditch.

What happened during the two days of heavy battle was still a confusion. The Bulgarians, despite being heavily outnumbered, courageously

---

1. Treaty of Brest-Litovsk was signed between the Bolshevik government in Russia and the Central Powers in March 1918. It ended the Russian participation in the war.

held on until dark on the first day, but it was clear they would be out-flanked on the second. The terrain was mountainous, muddy and cold. On the second day, the British were amazed to discover that the enemy was fleeing. Outraged at what they considered to be gross cowardice, the Allies pursued them and it all ended in a bloody rout. When the Bulgarians finally turned and stood their ground, the British were so brave under intensive fire that the French awarded them a collective Croix de Guerre – a rare distinction. They all had a favourite theory about why the Bulgarians retreated when they did.

Another evening, completely at his ease with a glass of wine in his hand, Henrys entertained them once again with tales from his own illustrious career. He was a veteran of many a colonial war. Stroking his moustache, he told them how he had spent most of his time in French Algeria and never expected to leave it. In 1912, he had participated in the French conquest of Morocco[2] by leading several thrilling cavalry charges. He loved it. He was a very good soldier and an insightful one. He liked nothing better than to describe fighting Berber tribesmen in the Zaian War.[3] His companions, having heard these stories many times, nevertheless, humoured the older man. They were all in their cups by then and liked to imagine themselves fighting on horseback, their swords hacking away at the enemy.

Then Henrys recounted how in the midst of all that entertainment, he was dragged away to fight the Germans on the Western Front in July 1916. That had been a very serious time. He had never seen anything so futile and chilling as the trenches. He thought nothing could be worse, but then, as they knew, he was pulled away again and given command of the French Army of the Orient on the Salonika Front.

His friends had heard it all before, but this time Henrys told them he considered Dobro Pole the most important battle of his life. It was the final blow. It finished the Germans on the Eastern Front. That victory

---

2. Morocco had become a French protectorate in 1912. Resident-General Louis-Hubert Lyautey sought to extend French influence eastwards through the Middle Atlas mountains towards French Algeria. This was opposed by the Zaian confederation of Berber tribes 1914-21. The French were forced to withdraw troops to fight in WW1, but left a holding force in place. The fighting was resumed in 1920.
3. The Zaian War was part of the French conquest of North Africa 1914-1921.

and the massive influx of American soldiers to the Allied war effort, forced the Germans to surrender in the West. Dobra Pole could truly be said to have been the last push in the East that helped to end the war.

Strutt mused a lot over this during the idle days watching the sun fall on the snowy landscape. The whole war had been so complex. There had been so many variables, so many twists and turns. The Bulgarians were ferocious fighters. They should have held out longer at Dobro Pole, but they sent word their German allies couldn't send more reinforcements and even more distressing news, that their army had revolted against their monarchy at home in Sofia. In fact, Strutt was told the Bulgarian army had largely disintegrated. The people had run out of the will to fight anymore. Strutt spent some time pondering this. The Bulgarians were good fighters, but he also knew how erratic and emotional they were. Given the right motivation, they might not stay down for long. The situation could quickly change.

All day Strutt had been feeling low. He looked out the window at the moonlight night. The River Marica was in icy flood, but their train tracks were well above it. As far as he could see there was nothing but dreary swampland and blasted trees. What did the future hold? He couldn't get his head around it.

He did laugh wryly the night they spent playing bridge. He, Henrys, Murat and Du Tilly played. Vadrot preferred to read. They gambled with Austrian crowns which were now valued at about one English penny each. Du Tilly was the worse player. In fact, arguably he was the worst player on Earth, which is why they all took turns having him as a partner. It was only fair. What a fool that little man was, he thought fondly. Luckily, he would be leaving them at Bucharest, but then they would need another bridge partner.

They passed Adrianople and continued through snow-covered mountains until evening when they pulled into Philippopolis. They all got out to stretch their legs along the bleak platform which had been cleared of snow. Henrys quietly told them this was where the British and Allied prisoners of war were mostly confined. 'Not a healthy spot, I would imagine,' said Murat grimacing as he took a good look around; his cigarette smoke streaming away from his hand. They all knew that thousands of soldiers, not just their own, had died in these dank hills from disease, starvation and cold.

Philippopolis, since called Plovdiv, was once a large and beautiful city built originally by Phillip II of Macedonia. Over the centuries it had lost its former glory and dwindled into dusty buildings and dirty streets. Strutt noticed a few ragged people queuing around a stall selling what looked like muddy vegetables. The pavements were broken and despair permeated the air. Strutt suddenly had a flash of memory of how colourful the market place used to be and quickly shut the door in his head. He and Florrie had been here once a long time ago. He had forgotten.

The next morning, they arrived at Sofia at 04.00 in freezing fog. They rose late and after a comfortable breakfast when a weak sun came out, they were alerted to visitors. Strutt, Vadrot and Murat left the train to be greeted by a Guard of Honour consisting of a score of black Algerian soldiers wrapped in grubby-looking great coats. General Chretien, the French commander of the Allied troops of Occupation was in charge. Strutt was not impressed.

After the usual courtesies, the guard was dismissed and Chretien offered to drive them around the town. Strutt asked to be taken to Colonel Napier, the British Attaché, as he had a letter for him from General Sir Tom Bridges. Vadrot and Murat decided to walk about the town and meet up with him later.

Colonel Napier greeted him formally in his rather grand office and offered him a chair and coffee. He inquired about the journey without much interest while he opened the letter Strutt had brought him. Napier was a dark-haired man with a genial smile, pale blue eyes and rather long face. He was probably in his late thirties. His heavily curtained windows overlooked a square full of snow, slush and sparse trees. Strutt had not met him before. He flicked the letter onto his desk. 'General Bridges does not think much of the Bulgarians, does he?' Napier was amused. Strutt was not. 'The Bulgars aren't really bad chaps, you know, when you get to know them.'

Strutt gave him a hard stare. He was angry. 'Pardon me, if I am not all sympathy,' replied Strutt stiffly. 'They killed a lot of our men before retreating and afterwards they killed a lot more. It will be a little time before I can look upon them with any affection.'

Napier just laughed at Strutt's starched attitude. 'It's true they might have surrendered at once, but they tell me their orders were to retreat. In any case, the war is over, Colonel.' He stood and with a smiling gesture invited him to have a drink and then some lunch. Strutt decided then and there that Napier was too lax. He was not a serious player and should be replaced – and so he was shortly thereafter. In Strutt's opinion, the war might be over, but a hard line with the volatile Bulgarians would be needed for some time. Fortunately, he was lunching with General Chretien and the others and didn't have to bear this fool company. He took his leave. He wasn't ready, like some, to walk away from the war without a care. It was far too early for that.

Chapter Two

February 7, 1919
Sofia

The five companions all had lunch at a passable restaurant in the centre of Sofia which General Chretien had selected. It had a charming, rather threadbare pre-war atmosphere which appealed to Strutt and the food was really quite tasty. First a delicious Tarator soup, made with cucumber, yoghurt and spices was served along with thick wedges of brown bread. This was followed by a platter of Sarmi, little oblong fried cakes made with minced meat and rice and wrapped in sauerkraut. Strutt had to laughingly refuse the Bougatsa at the end. He was full.

Murat and Du Tilly spent most of lunch explaining to an incredulous Chretien the difficulties they had getting small scale maps of northern Greece, let alone for the Dobro Pole effort. Chretien found it hard to believe the Allies spent their first months in Salonika sending out surveyors to make maps and find likely spots to drill water holes. Had there been nothing there at all?

Finally Henrys butted in. He spoke grandly, sitting back in his chair replete with good food. 'Everyone moans about the difficulties. No doubt our friend here, he said, looking at Strutt, could make us weep over the problems of directing fighting men who spoke few known languages. The real sadness, the tragedy, was that the Eastern Front cost so much in men, mules and horses. We will always regret that, but at least it ended in victory.' The men all banged their glasses on the table to show their agreement.

Later, they strolled by the new Alexander Nevsky Cathedral. There was a plaque in front commemorating Russian soldiers who died liberating Bulgaria forever from the Ottomans in 1877-78. Du Tilly asked Henrys how he supposed people would commemorate their war? Henrys thought about it for a while and decided one monument here and there would not be enough. No, war cemeteries would mark their war – lots of them. There should be a war memorial in every village and town. People should never forget the sacrifice demanded of them during the years 1914-18. Strutt thought this would be true. They were saying that more people had died in their war than in all other wars in history combined. It was hard to take in. They walked back to the train and boarded it in silence.

The next day happened to be Strutt's forty-fifth birthday. To honour this august occasion, Henrys decided it would be suitable to finish off all the wine they had liberated from Salonika, especially as they would be leaving the train the following day. Dinner therefore was marginally better than usual and Vadrot even managed to order up a sachertorte of sorts with a candle on top which made Strutt laugh in amazement; none of them had seen one of these in an age. He was surprised and touched as well after receiving their extravagant praise for all his endeavours. Henrys toasted him as 'possibly the best battlefield linguist I have ever had the pleasure of working with.' Strutt stood and told them they had all done it together; that they should all be proud of succeeding against such appalling odds; and he thanked them for making him the gift of their friendship which he would never forget.

Captain Vadrot, whom Strutt never liked, despite his often hilarious jokes and anecdotes, tonight raised his glass and said gruffly that as their soldiering days were now over, they should drink to the hope of a happy future. Murat, the youngest of them, perked up from a slight drink-induced befuddlement on the sofa to remind them that they were not home yet. They may still have to battle their way through. He was booed by all.

Strutt, who was half asleep by then, nearly snarled 'Let's hope they don't make a bodge of the final Treaty so we have to do it all over again!', but thought better of it. It had been a fine birthday celebration; best not to spoil it. He had heard nothing on the subject in any case.

By mid-afternoon the next day, they had arrived at Rustchuk, a God-forsaken village on the Danube. Here they disembarked the train and were rendered instantly speechless by the freezing air. It had got much colder. Strutt's leg began to protest.

A shell burst had badly damaged his left leg back in September 1914 when he had led his battalion in its first engagement at Vieille Chapelle right at the beginning of the war. He'd been invalided out with concussion as well. It had taken months to fully recuperate. While he was recovering he was able to take up a job with MI3, the new Intelligence outfit, and there he found his true metier. It turned out he had a talent for gathering together and making sense of disparate intelligent reports. Furthermore, he could digest the information and quickly produce concise options for action. This talent was recognised by his confederates. He had wound up in Salonika because of his language skills and the fear that the coming battle at Dobro Pole would be a mess without his sharpness in navigating problems. He'd never worked so hard.

Before them an old fishing vessel, which was to be their transport across the Danube, stood a good sixty yards away, separated from the quayside by frozen chunks of packed ice. Fortunately, before they themselves turned into frozen chunks, a group of porters came up, took their luggage from them and proceeded to nimbly walk across the ice floe towards the ship. Strutt grimaced. Murat had the right idea. They were going to have to fight their way through. He then scouted around for a fallen tree limb to use as a walking stick. The others did the same.

By the time they were ready to cross, the porters had reached the ship and come back to help them. So, clutching a porter's arm with one hand and their walking sticks with the other, they managed to stay upright as they stepped carefully over the shards and hummocks of ice. They all had on heavy boots, but even so, the ice was treacherous.

They were half-way across when Murat, thinking he could manage alone, lost his footing and one leg fell through a crack into the freezing water. He yelled and threw himself across the ice, grabbing at anything to keep from falling further. His porter snatched at his belt to hold him up.

Fortunately, it all ended well. Four porters carried Murat to the ship and the others took even more care following them. The ship itself had icy decks and a rude interior, but it ferried them all across the river to Giurgiu, a small town in Romania which had obviously seen some serious fighting. Buildings were damaged, windows were broken and shell holes were blasted liberally through walls and roofs. As a consequence, their billet was spartan. They were taken to an ancient wooden guest house where the food was barely tolerable. At least the beds were dry, but they were so cold none of them got much sleep. Strutt covered his legs with his great coat.

The next morning, Du Tilly was to leave them to take up his new duties in Bucharest. His job, as they all knew, was to be liaison officer between General Berthelot,[1] commander of the Romanian Army and General Patey,[2] who commanded the French Army of Occupation. These officers' headquarters were at opposite ends of the town, so Du Tilly would not be overworked. Strutt, rather unkindly, thought him perfect for the job.

The little Frenchman had brushed his uniform and made himself look quite smart. Henrys was very kind to him. As Strutt looked on, he told him he had no doubt he would do a splendid job and promised to mention to General Berthelot, when he met him, what a superb job Du Tilly had done at Salonika. Du Tilly bursting with pleasure and pride replied it had been an honour to serve with them, saluted and departed.

Shortly after that, a small 'hairy-heeled'[3] Bulgarian came in to announce that their transport had arrived to take them on to Calugareni. It consisted of two bullock- drawn sleighs. In the end, they walked most of the way along the snow-covered road just to keep warm. The temperature was −2°F. Finally after a couple of hours, they arrived at Calugareni and found a sedan car waiting in the little main square to take them the rest of the way to Bucharest. It was only 30 more kilometres. Unfortunately, the driver of the car was an insane Frenchman who drove like a madman. The car skidded all over the icy roads and twice they barely avoided a crash. It was a harrowing experience and afterwards Strutt let Vadrot scare the driver with his own brand of terrifying retribution.

So it was that they arrived at General Berthelot's residence at 13.05 feeling the worse for wear, but they all cheered up wonderfully with the warmth of General Berthelot's welcome and some delicious mulled wine offered as a restorative.

General Berthelot was a great bear of a man in his late fifties with grey hair, grey moustache and goatee. He welcomed them jovially. Strutt had

---

1. General Berthelot (1861-1931), Chief of the General Staff under Joffre, Commander of the French forces on the Western Front at the beginning of the war. Later commander of the Romanian Army.
2. General Patey, Commander of the French Second Groupement (16th Colonial Division and the 30th Metropolitan) stationed at Bucharest.
3. Strutt's slang term for anyone he considered to be of 'primitive ancestry.'

heard quite a lot about him and was fully aware that Berthelot's good looks and larger than life personality could captivate as well as intimidate when required. He was a very powerful man. He had been Chief of the General Staff under Joffre and reputedly had done an excellent job. In 1916, he was put in charge of retraining and reorganising the Romanian Army into a respectable fighting force. He was now their commander.

Berthelot gave them a very good lunch consisting of one of the best sarmale Strutt had ever tasted. These were cabbage rolls of rice, minced pork, sliced bacon, chopped vegetables all smothered in parsley and mint. They burst with flavour. This was served with mamaliga, a type of corn-flour bread. For dessert there was a pancake filled with pieces of apple and raisins and drizzled with honey. The comrades so enjoyed Berthelot's company that they were reluctant to leave in mid-afternoon, but time was pressing.

Later, when Strutt was told that Berthelot was the real ruler of Romania as he had managed to put the Queen in his pocket, he wasn't surprised. But on the other hand, he thought with some amusement, given what he knew of that lady, it was also possible that the Queen had captivated and subjugated Berthelot! He would soon see.

Chapter Three

February 9, 1919
Bucharest

The four remaining comrades were taken to the Hotel Athenee in the centre of Bucharest, which was modern, steam-heated and thankfully undamaged. Unfortunately, before they were routed, the Germans had unscrewed and removed the pipes leading to the toilets, but rudimentary measures had been instituted to ameliorate the situation. They occupied themselves with making courtesy calls on the town's top military officials and writing their names in the King and Queen's book at the town hall. Strutt was upset that all the French troops he saw were still in their summer drill uniforms and had only fur caps. No wonder so many of them looked ill. That evening, he and General Henrys dined alone with General Berthelot in his very comfortable palace and later he went out alone with Vadrot and Murat for a more riotous experience in the town.

The next morning, something curious happened. Strutt went to pay another courtesy visit. This time to Sir George Barclay, the British Minister, who was preoccupied, but nevertheless stopped to greet him with extreme cordiality. Strutt was taken aback. Barclay had never before been more than stiffly formal with him. Did he know something he didn't? Strutt was non plussed, but left it at that. At 14.00 he received a summons to attend the Palace at Cotroceni. The Queen wished to see him. Strutt could think of no reason for the summons except Berthelot's recommendation, which pleased him. He looked forward to meeting her. A staff car drove him up.

The sprawling Cotroceni Palace was situated on a hill in the centre of Bucharest. It was not unattractive. Rebuilt in 1893 in the Romanian Renaissance style, characterised by firm overhanging roof lines and lots of pillars supporting baroque arches, it was set in lovely gardens. Strutt noticed a small stream running through it. He was received at once.

At that time, Queen Marie of Romania was forty-four years old and as vivacious and attractive as ever, maybe even more so. Under her dark hair, her wide blue eyes sparkled as she greeted him with great friendliness, reminding him of their last meeting in Munich in 1912. As the daughter of the Duke of Edinburgh, Queen Victoria's second son, she naturally spoke perfect English and was greatly interested in all the court gossip Strutt could tell her. He found her fascinating and as intelligent as he had been told. He knew that she was the real ruler of Romania and that it was rumoured that not all her children were her husband's, but he had not been prepared for her wit. She made him laugh in spite of himself.

Her husband, King Ferdinand and their daughter Princess Elizabeth, aged twenty-five, appeared for a few minutes, but were not invited to join them. Later Princess Ileana, aged ten, came in and was allowed to remain. She was a pretty child. Strutt and the Queen chatted for two hours. During their discussions, Her Majesty gave the impression that she was anxious to marry off Princess Elizabeth to Prince Alexander of Serbia. Strutt was emollient. 'I spoke in his praise and was as tactful as I could be,' he wrote in his diary. But it finally came out that the Princess must be twice the height and weight of the Prince and this put the Queen into fits of laughter. Strutt joined her. It was too silly.

He would not hear for some months that soon this compelling Queen would insist on journeying to Paris to attend the Peace Conference at Versailles with the Romanian delegation. Finding that things were not going well for her country, she would shock many officials by waving her ministers aside and leading the negotiations herself. It was acknowledged that she used her tremendous charm, beauty and wit to great effect at both the Conference table and behind the scenes.

The result would be that she would leave France with a trainload of supplies for Romania's relief and later in the year, the Conference would award Romania all the territory it had asked for (a 60 per cent enlargement) which included nearly the whole of Transylvania and an increase of ten million in population. It was a spectacular triumph for which her eldest son, later King Carol of Romania and a thoroughly bad hat, would never forgive her. She had usurped her husband's role and shown him to be the incompetent fool he was for all the world to see.

Before she dismissed Strutt that afternoon, the Queen, with an extravagant encomium, awarded him the Star of Romania (Officer) for his services during the war. Strutt was pleased. This was his first 'after dinner' or rather 'after tea' decoration. He kissed her hand in farewell with some of his old charm. He felt honoured to know such a remarkable woman. Furthermore, there was no doubt in his mind that she had netted Berthelot, not the other way around!

The following day the now four comrades, minus du Tilly continued their journey to Venice via Belgrade and Zagreb. Another special train had been laid on for them, but it was delayed for some hours. They had to return to General Patey's for an early lunch and finally got away at 13.25 after a final farewell to a lachrymose du Tilly.

Coming away, their general impression of Bucharest was that the people were desperate for coal and food. Prices were so high that only a few days before their arrival, there had been food riots in front of the palace. A kind of martial law had been proclaimed to which no one paid the slightest attention. The Queen had described it as 'a little difficulty, soon mended.' This was doubtful.

According to both the Queen and Berthelot, there was no Bolshevism in evidence. Bucharest, itself had not been much damaged by the numerous air raids during the War. The streets and fine buildings still had a respectable air about them. Strutt thought the officers of the Romanian army left a bad impression with few exceptions. The men on the other hand appeared to be good, but except for the Royal Guards, they were badly in need of clothing.

Chapter Four

February 10, 1919
Orsova

After Craiova, they eventually arrived at Orsova. The Serbian guard holding the station, beamed at the sight of a British uniform. The station was full of passenger trains which had been held up by the snow and Romanian incompetence. To be fair, the Hungarians had stolen most of the Romanian engines back in 1915, so they weren't doing that badly. They left Orsova at 14.20 and ran well past the Iron Gates where the Danube was a moving sea of ice floes, passed Trajan's Gate and Herkules-Bad and reached Temesvar at 19.55 in time for dinner.

For once, the dinner was surprisingly good. The czardas band played divinely and the town blazed with light. There were no visible signs of hardship anywhere, but Strutt was told there was a great shortage of food under the surface of things. What a pity, thought Strutt, who had quite cheered up at what looked like a fairly prosperous place.

After dinner, General Jouinot-Gambetta, a great friend of Strutt's, who so brilliantly commanded the French cavalry of the Arme d'Afrique (the French North African army) in Macedonia, joined them for the trip back to the railway station. He was going to Belgrade as well. With flashing eyes, he told them a great tale about his recent activities in Greece.

Sadly, later that night, long after their departure, the train somehow became overheated and the bugs and lice emerged to take their toll. It was impossible to sleep. The next morning, they arrived at Panesova on the Theiss River in the Banat. This area, formed by the great Pannonian Basin, was a region that straddled Central and Eastern Europe. It lay between three rivers: the Danube to the south, the Theiss in the west, and Mures to the north. On the eastern border lay the Southern Carpathians. After Austria lost it in 1918, it was divided between Romania, Hungary and Serbia, but in truth it had always been a region of shifting peoples.

Strutt opened his weary eyes and looked out the window. He could hardly see anything for the frost on the window pane, but he could make out that the temperature was still sub-zero and the snow deep. Mercifully, the temperature in the train had gone back to its usual cold and the bugs had retreated. His leg was quiescent. Shortly, the conductor came along and told them to report the train could go no further due to the ice and that they would have to walk the rest of the way to their ship if they wanted to cross the Theiss.

This time the steamer, one of Admiral Troubridge's Danube fleet, was only 30 yards from the shore. Strutt and Henrys looked for handy branches to use as walking sticks and strode confidently onto the ice. Henrys shouted at Murat not to drown himself this time. It was hard going, but they all got through to the ship without incident. Jouinot-Gambetta immediately made them all a splendid rum punch at the bar which was much appreciated.

Strutt was very curious about Admiral Troubridge's staff officer, who was there to meet them. He was a rather heavy-set Englishman in his middle forties. He couldn't help noticing that his naval tunic was covered with decorations of every army except the British – three rows of medals – and yet he admitted in conversation to never having seen a shot fired. Strutt thought this strange, if true, and nearly asked him about it, but decided in the end not to enquire. The war threw up many exceptional stories, not all of them worth hearing. He wasn't in the mood.

That night, again, it was almost impossible to sleep. Their cabins were perfectly adequate. He shared his with Murat who had the top bunk. It was the noise. The frightful crashes and bangs of the ice falling in cascades over the ship's bows made them feel that they were sleeping in a ball bearing factory. Could the ship take the strain, he wondered? Before dinner, from the great cabin on the main deck, he'd seen several wrecked Austrian monitors lying on their sides encased in ice. Florrie would be so disappointed if he survived the whole war only to die here, crushed in the ice on the bloody Theiss! Finally, he got a few hours sleep and in the morning he was relieved to find their ship had made steady progress. They reached Belgrade by 12.00 the next day.

Chapter Five

February 12–19, 1919
Belgrade

T he next five days were taken up with military duties in and around Belgrade. The city, situated where the Sava River meets the Danube, was still looking shell-shocked after the prolonged and desperate battle in 1915 when it was defeated by the Germans. In 1918 to the fierce joy of the citizenry, the country was liberated by French and Serbian troops under the command of Strutt's friend General Franchet d'Esperey and Crown Prince Alexander of Serbia. There had been some attempt at re-building, but not much.

Both Henrys and Strutt thought it expedient to reconnoitre the area for news on all fronts. The war might be over, but they weren't taking it for granted. Events were moving apace that might yet affect the Allied position at the Treaty table. Both of them made it their business to interview as many high-ranking officers and Embassy officials as possible.

Strutt even took the trouble to look up at an old friend of his, the Voivode[1] Mishitch, former Commander in Chief of the Royal Serbian Army and one of the greatest soldiers living. He was sixty-seven now with silver hair and bushy eyebrows, but his eyes still snapped with intelligence. He invited Strutt into his comfortable apartment in one of the gracious nineteenth century buildings left untouched by the bombs. He was delighted to see him. Visitors were fewer now that he was retired, but he still had his ear to the ground. Strutt was glad of it. He always enjoyed hearing Mishitch's opinion on world events. This time, he heard nothing he didn't know already. The Voivode was not unduly worried about the communists. He was far more concerned about rebuilding Serbia's economy now that the country had incorporated the Croats and Slovenes into a new and greater

---

1. Voivode is a Slavic term for a military commander in Central, Eastern and Southern Europe originating in the Middle Ages.

Kingdom of Serbia the year before.[2] He didn't see how it would work. They enjoyed a warm chat about this and other things for some time. Strutt told him he would come again before he left.

The next afternoon, the comrades all had an interesting time at a *'Prise d'Armes'* (military prize giving) given in the beautiful ballroom at the Old Palace. One side of this building had been badly damaged during the war, but the entrance hall and the ballroom were still as glittering as ever. Huge white Venetian glass chandeliers cast their light on the lemon-yellow walls interspersed with white marble statues and carvings. Strutt was impressed by the Serb's good taste. It was a lovely room.

The Voivode Mishitch received the 'Grand Cordon of the Legion d'Honour'. The new medal had not yet arrived, so General Henrys presented him with his own. Jouinot-Gambetta received the 'Grand Officer' award and many 'Chevaliers' were also awarded to Serbian and French officers along with numerous Croix de Guerre and 'Palmes.' All this was watched by a large and enthusiastic crowd.

When he got back to his room that evening, Strutt was disgusted to find that much of his kit had been looted and all his cigarettes. He was reduced to one pair of pyjamas, two shirts and the one pair of plus-four knickerbockers which he was wearing. Luckily, the thief hadn't taken his dress uniform. Somewhere, he would have to find replacements. He, of course, did not suspect the batman who had been assigned to him by the hotel!

The next day, he had to avert a potentially very embarrassing discovery. It was a complete surprise and nearly caught him on the back foot. The Voivode Mishitch had sent for him that morning to discuss a delicate matter he'd forgotten to mention when they'd talked before. Barclays Bank in London had sent him various receipted bills from Eton College. He was confused. Why was this? Unbeknownst to him, GHQ British Salonika Force had sent Mishitch's youngest son to Eton as a compliment and had paid all expenses. GHQ had been at pains to conceal this fact from the Voivode who thought his son was on a scholarship. Strutt, thinking quickly, told Mishitch that the receipts had been sent in error by Barclays and that he should burn them at once. Later, Strutt told General

---

2. The Kingdom of Serbia was renamed the Kingdom of Yugoslavia in 1929.

Henrys, whose idea it was, that it was very lucky that it was he who was sent for and not someone who wasn't in the picture.

After lunch, the five of them – Henrys, Jouinot-Gambetta, Vadrot, Murat and Strutt continued their journey via the Sava and Danube rivers to Semlin Town where they boarded Prince Alexander of Serbia's luxurious private sleeping car which had been lent to them by a grateful prince. It was a gorgeous vehicle with velvet cushions and every comfort. They passed Vukovar at 6.00 and Strutt remembered the Oettingens, old friends who had once lived there. Before he could stop himself he was wondering where they might be and whether he would ever see them again. He quickly brushed the thought away. Remembering the old days just brought pain.

On the 19th, they arrived at Zagreb station to find the splendid figure of Admiral Sir Ernest Troubridge himself waiting to greet them in full fig with medals gleaming. He was full of cheery enthusiasm. Strutt was honoured to meet him. Here was an outstanding example of courage overcoming adversity.

Before the war Troubridge had been immensely well thought of in naval circles and had risen to becoming Private Secretary to the 1st Lord of the Admiralty, serving Winston Churchill and his predecessor. He was considered a born leader. In January 1913, he was given command of the Mediterranean cruiser squadron under Admiral Milne and all looked very promising indeed. However, in confusing circumstances in August 1914, he was blamed for not pursuing two German cruisers. This led to a court-martial in September of that year from which he was honourably exonerated, but the damage was done. He never had another sea-going command. He took it on the chin. In 1915 he was given command of the naval detachments and flotillas on the Danube during the Balkan campaign, winning the respect of the Crown Prince of Serbia. After the war in 1919 he was made full Admiral and served on the Danube Commission, eventually becoming its president. Strutt admired his grit.

They all breakfasted together. General Henrys and Jouinot-Gambetta couldn't stop heaping praise on the British navy and asking questions. Too soon, they had to excuse themselves and say goodbye. It was time to re-embark their train for Fiume. They were getting close to the end of their combined journey.

Chapter Six

February 19th Evening
Fiume

Hlgh above the port of Fiume beautiful views opened out over the Adriatic. The snow was disappearing as the train descended by long zigzags towards the sea, which looked rather bleak in its winter guise. Strutt suddenly remembered the last time he had been here it had been in spring. What would spring bring this time, he wondered sadly.

Fiume had a long history of conflict between Italy, Serbia and Hungary. It was then an enormously valuable deep water port and they all wanted it. After the colleagues arrived at 16.15, Henrys and Strutt walked down to a place overlooking the harbour. The wind had calmed and a weak sun shone through the clouds. Henrys put his hands behind his back and blew out his chest. 'You British did a damn fine job keeping supplies from getting to the enemy here. It can't have been easy.' 'No,' replied Strutt. 'Our frigates paid a heavy price to the German U-boats, but it had to be done. The trouble is that too many people died as a consequence.' Henry agreed. 'We will have to put that fact behind us, I think. People will now be looking to the future. Later they will look back.' Strutt knew this was probably true, but doubted he would ever want to reminisce over anything so grotesque. He planned to just bury the whole bloody thing.

After a rough night in a bad hotel, the party left for the final leg of their journey to Venice in four comfortable Fiat staff cars. The road across the Istrian Peninsula was quite beautiful. This was the famous Karst Plateau, a region of limestone, dolomite and gypsum full of underground drainage systems, sinkholes and caves. It used to be covered in oak, but the Venetians had cut most of them down centuries ago for pillars to build their island city. Now the view above Fiume to Abbazia was framed by thickets of pine trees that lined the road. The weak sun flickered through them like a silent movie as they drove along. When they neared

Trieste a mist and then a drizzle set in. They descended by long and easy curves to the town, where they arrived at the headquarters of the Duke of Aosta who was commanding the Italian Army of Occupation. It was late morning. The Duke was away, but they were entertained by his aide, the Italian General Count Pettiti, who couldn't do enough for them.

After lunch he invited them to see Miramare Castle, the former residence of the unlucky Emperor Maximilian of Mexico. He was very insistent and urged them to agree. It was just a short drive away and shouldn't be missed. Until lately it had been the home of the Archduchess Maria Josefa, mother of the Emperor Karl of Austria.

When they got there, Strutt thought the situation by the sea truly lovely. The three- story castle was really a very comfortable mansion with a crenulated tower at one end. Unfortunately, he was repelled by the interior. He wrote his disgust in his diary that the inside was furnished in the most revolting middle-class taste. Dark curtains, brown furniture with endless overstuffed cushions, little tables full of knick-knacks, what-nots brimming with photo frames and vases erupting with peacock feathers covered every surface.

The only objects of interest were two fine portraits of Archduke Maximilian, Emperor Franz Joseph's younger brother, and his wife Charlotte of Belgium. Painted in 1865, they showed the proud pair in their regalia as Emperor and Empress of Mexico. Strutt remembered that tragic folly and shook his head. If ever envy and ambition had overrode good sense, that was surely a prime example. Maximilian was executed by firing squad and poor Carlota went mad. They didn't stay long.

In the early evening, they boarded the train to Venice where they arrived just before midnight. It was a short journey. In the dark, Strutt thought with relief that Venice looked like she always did, mysterious and welcoming. The French Admiral's picket boat conveyed the whole party to the Hotel Daniele where sumptuous rooms awaited them. Everything worked from the lighting to the lavatories. Strutt felt his shoulders relax. This was normality. This was bliss. He felt the whole ghastly mess was nearly over. His plan was to stay one night in Venice, then proceed as ordered to Taranto by way of Rome. There he would take another ship to Constantinople where his superior General Tom Bridges was now stationed. It seemed mad to go in reverse, so to speak, when he was so close to Paris, but these were his orders. He must make one final report.

After that he would be free to meet Florrie in Paris and go home. He wrote her a long letter before he slept. Lord, how he was looking forward to seeing the old girl. Everything would be all right then.

After a delightful breakfast the next morning in the dining room, they all went out into the sunshine to view the sights. The air was crystal clear. Strutt was saddened to see Piazza San Marco full of debris. St. Mark's itself was still sandbagged and in the Doge's Palace everything had been removed for safe keeping, including the four proud bronze horses on top. Mercifully, there were no signs of aerial bombardment as was almost invariably the case elsewhere and the lagoon was as serene as ever. They lunched with Admiral Ratier, the French Commander of the North Adriatic. While there, Strutt made arrangements for his journey on to Taranto.

That evening, the colleagues had a very good last dinner together. All but Strutt were leaving later that night on the train to Paris and home. What a time they had had. Vadrot, blowing a smoke ring into the air, asked Strutt what his plans were for the future and Strutt told him he planned to go home where he would probably be given a battalion to command. Vadrot laughed. 'Your talents will be wasted, *mon ami*. Anyone can run a battalion in peacetime.'

Strutt replied that he would be content. He'd had enough excitement to last a very long time. The rest of them were just looking forward to seeing their families again. At 22.00, with real regret, Strutt parted from his French colleagues. He would never forget them – Generals Henrys and Jouinot-Gambetta nor the very capable ADCs Vadrot and Murat. He was proud to have known them and he meant it.

Feeling a sense of anti-climax, Strutt went back to the bar for a nightcap and saw his reflection in the mirror. Lord, he looked old, he thought. He was forty-five. His brown hair was starting to go grey and his forehead and hazel eyes had harsh lines around them that weren't put there by laughter. He'd still kept his erect figure, thank God. All the fighting and shortage of food had been good for something. He asked for a whisky.

Strutt had been a serving officer since before the Boer War in 1900. His forté was an ability to cut rapidly to the core of a problem and succinctly persuade people to work together to an effective solution. He could do this fluently in French, German and Italian and well enough in several other languages. This made him very valuable, given the lack of such men. It sometimes annoyed him that due to this ability, he was still only a lieutenant colonel, but they needed to be able to move him around quickly. Most of the time he didn't mind, he preferred life as a staff officer. He was too impatient and his temper in the face of stupidity was often too short to control, but it got things done.

Now, standing at the bar, sipping his whisky, he thought 'what now?' It would take years to rebuild the cities and industries, he mused. He and Florrie would have to start again at a new posting. Really, it was too hard to think about right now, but he knew everything would be fine once he got home. He and Florrie always landed on their feet. With that steadying thought, he took himself off to bed. He thanked God again that it was all over.

In the late morning, after a surprisingly good sleep and breakfast which left him in a much better frame of mind, Strutt said his goodbyes to Marcello, the concierge, whom he remembered fondly from former visits before the war and walked out the door heading for the steam cutter. A porter preceded him carrying his bags. He was nearly there, when he heard Marcello running after him calling him to wait. He was waving a telegram with orders for Strutt to remain another day. Urgent orders, it said were soon to arrive from Padua. This did not sound good. He must wait.

Chapter Seven

York House, Windsor Great Park, December 1918

The Christmas decorations were fluttering in Windsor High Street as Prince Sixtus' car made the turn into the town. The young prince, now thirty years old, was an officer in the Belgian Army, but beyond that he was a Bourbon-Parma and his loyalty was first of all to his House. He and his younger brother Prince Xavier, who accompanied him, had come to ask for help for their sister and brother-in-law, the Emperor and Empress of Austria-Hungary. Both of them were of average height, reed slim and dressed in the green tunic of their regiment. They were on leave.

After the upsetting and mortifying interview they had a few weeks previously with the French Prime Minister Briand, who summarily threw them out, they were not sanguine about the success of their visit today. Indeed, they were embarrassed to be here, but needs must. Their sister, the Empress Zita was counting on them to find her family a place of safety.

Sixtus had written ahead to the Lord Chamberlain asking for an interview with His Majesty King George and he was moderately encouraged when he received a polite note giving a date and time. Their Majesties did not reside full-time at Windsor Castle, but were mainly to be found at York House, an uninspiring villa situated on the outskirts of the park one or two miles away. They had heard that the very retiring royal couple preferred to live unostentatiously when they got the chance, but they were not quite prepared for the smallness of the Victorian house when they arrived. A miserable thin rain greeted them as they stepped out of the car.

The butler took their cloaks, hats and gloves and a footman showed them to a rather fussy small salon over full with furniture and framed pictures. There was a good fire, however, which cheered them. They sat down on over- upholstered chairs and waited. Xavier looked nervously at his brother. This was their last chance.

Shortly, without any fanfare, Queen Mary walked into the room followed by His Majesty. Both men stood and bowed reverently. Queen Mary was dressed unfashionably in a floor-length, dark blue woollen gown with a pearl choker and another strand of pearls hanging down her bodice. Most women they knew were wearing the shorter skirts which had become fashionable during the war, so she seemed even more remote to them. The King was in a tweed jacket. Sixtus introduced his brother. The King greeted them both graciously and invited them to sit. He was reminded that he had met them before in 1916. The Queen offered tea.

After the King inquired about their mother and various noble relations, Prince Sixtus got around to the purpose of their visit. Putting his tea cup down carefully, he began to describe what a difficult time his sister and the Emperor Karl were enduring since the Armistice. Things had got so bad that three months ago they had been forced to leave Schoenbrunn Palace to seek safety in the countryside.

The King nodded his head. He had heard they were now at their hunting lodge near the Hungarian border. Sixtus told him that was correct. They were at Eckartsau Castle. A nice place to visit in the autumn for the sport, but not so desirable in winter. It was not large and at the moment the whole Court was there in vastly overcrowded conditions. Worse, the Empress had written him that food was shortly to become a problem.

The King rubbed his forehead and asked what the political situation in Vienna might be.

Prince Sixtus, then sat back in his chair and proceeded to tell him. The former government had fallen and a Provisional clique was trying to hold things together. How long it would last was not easy to say. Tens of thousands of deserters and criminals of all sorts who had been infected with Communism were flooding through the countryside. Many of them were Austrian soldiers angry with the Emperor for getting them into the war in the first place. At this point, Sixtus faltered. He was trying hard to contain his emotions, sensing an impassioned plea would discomfort his audience.

The King stopped him to ask who was protecting the Imperial Family. He felt sure the Provisional Government would make it a priority to maintain and guard them.

Sixtus looked at his shoes and told them that was one of the difficulties. The blunt truth was that the Provisional government had abandoned them. He looked up and their Majesties could see the anguish in his face. Prince Xavier was grimly staring at the fire.

It was all right for the moment, he told them. His sister had so far managed to secure food supplies, but there were so many people dependent on her, it was hard to keep up. She was fearful that her sources of supply would soon stop. She often heard guns in the night and they only had a few policemen with them for protection.

Queen Mary was appalled. She remembered Karl and Zita had come to their coronation in 1911. Such a sweet young couple they were then, so much in love. She asked Prince Sixtus for news of the Emperor. Surely he had things in hand?

Sixtus, paused, visibly upset and gestured to Xavier to continue. He eagerly sat forward and told Their Majesties that their brother-in-law, the Emperor had not been well this last year. He had suffered a series of small heart attacks and had been in bed. Their sister was in charge of everything. He then made what he considered might be the ultimate persuader and told them she was pregnant again.

Now the King was distressed. He asked how many children had they got now? Xavier told him there were five at the moment and another was on the way. Prince Otto was the eldest. The King laughed. What a fertile lot the Bourbon-Parmas were. He asked Sixtus how many children did his father have in the end?

Sixtus replied that there were twenty-four of them by two marriages.

The King was quiet for a few moments. He said he would like to help the Emperor and his family. He remembered well that Karl had tried to end the war when he ascended the throne in 1916. The attempt was to his credit, but it failed. However, and he looked steadily at Sixtus, the Emperor didn't help anyone by writing letters to the French behind his German allies' back, did he? At this, Sixtus bowed his head as well he might. The King was clearly well-briefed on what was being called 'The Sixtus Affair.' This was the disastrous attempt by the Emperor to end the war in 1916 using Prince Sixtus as his intermediary with the French.

Sixtus looked up at the King. He wasn't going to apologise for such a desperate throw. The carnage and suffering in the Austro-Hungarian

Empire was just terrible at the time. People were starving and they still were.

The King looked at Queen Mary in silence for a moment, and then asked where they were staying? Prince Xavier said they were at the Belgian Embassy.

In that case, said the King standing, their request for help would be considered, but they must realize that the British government couldn't possibly send troops into Austria to aid an Emperor who was their sworn enemy until a few weeks ago. The whole idea was preposterous. The war only ended in November. In fact, some would say their coming to ask for help was an outrageous impertinence. The King looked at them coolly.

The two princes trembled at this, still clutching their napkins, but before they could say anything, the King's mood softened. He sighed. He understood the urgency of their need and didn't consider it impertinent. In times of danger, families do what they must. He would talk to the Prime Minister and see what could be done, if anything.

Prince Sixtus was overcome by this show of sympathy. He could have wept, but contained himself and thanked the King for his great generosity to even consider helping the Habsburgs. He knew it was not an easy decision, but he was, in fact, their last hope. The King looked at him sharply at this unwelcome news and told him he could promise nothing, but he would look into it. The three men shook hands and the Princes bowed over Queen Mary's hand in farewell. The King assured them they would be contacted soon. He suspected time was short.

After the two princes took their leave with profuse thanks, King George sat down again and asked his wife what she made of it all. He then helped himself to another scone. The Princes had been too nervous to eat and he had been too tense. Mary looked at him with great tenderness. She knew him well. Before she could reply he reminded her how he hadn't been able to forgive himself for the fate of the Romanovs. What an atrocity. Who could have conceived that it would happen? If only Nicky had got them out early on. He could have helped them then, but by the time things became desperate, the political situation in England had become so anti-German, their own Royal House was under threat. That's why they changed their name from Saxe-Coburg-Gotha, if she remembered.

Queen Mary leaned over and patted his hand. The King was getting upset. He would think of a solution. No, they could not let another royal family be murdered in a basement, even if this time they were unrelated. The Habsburgs were good people and they too had five children.

The next morning the King summoned a very surprised Prime Minister and a plan was forged. This mission would require utmost discretion. They decided, after much thought that it would be best to send in just one man, someone with just the right qualifications. He could find out what needed to be done, formulate a plan and report back to London. No one else could be involved. A few weeks later, a suitable officer was selected and a top priority cipher was sent out to Constantinople. The game was on.

Chapter Eight

February 21, 1919
Venice

Strutt woke the next morning feeling groggy after a very uneasy night. What in hell could be in that telegram? What would the new orders be? Please God, let nothing stop him from getting to Paris as planned.

Without anything else to occupy him and to take his mind off a sense of foreboding, Strutt spent the day wandering the wintry canals of Venice. He was sad to see that sandbags were still surrounding the buildings in the cold, lonely piazzas. Few people were about. Every view, now in the daylight, looked beaten and weary, but even in her shabby state Venice still exuded an enticing dream of her former glories. He and Florrie had loved coming here, particularly in early June before it got too hot. The wind was becoming chilly, so eventually he turned up his collar and walked back to the Danieli, thinking of happier times. Had he really once hired a gondola and poled Florrie down the canals himself? How she would laughed. It had been another world. He decided to pick up a book in the hotel library to keep him company that evening.

At 14.00 the following day, Strutt was summoned to a private room by General Babington, the former Commander in Chief of Kitchener's old army, now the 29th Division, and his Chief of Staff, Brigadier General Pitt Taylor. They had newly arrived at the hotel. At the mere sight of them, Strutt's knew the news was going to be very bad. After the usual courtesies and curious glances offered by all parties, for Babington himself did not understand the reason behind his presence there, Babington handed Strutt an envelope. The message was from his Chief, Lieutenant General Sir Tom Bridges, Constantinople, and it read:

TOP SECRET
You will proceed at once to Eckartsau and give Emperor and Empress moral support of British Government. They are stated to be in danger of their lives, to be suffering great hardships and lack medical attention. Endeavour by every possible means to ameliorate their condition (signed) Lt General Tom Bridges.

Strutt was flabbergasted and Babington himself was amazed that a British officer would be given such a task. They all concluded that the 'Emperor' must be the Emperor of Austria. Strutt was outraged. Since when did their lot care what happened to the bloody Habsburgs? The war was over. He was on his way home. The whole idea was insane.

Babington told him the orders came direct from Downing Street. He was as surprised as Strutt, but nothing was to be done. He was terribly sorry. He looked dismayed.

Strutt was incandescent. What does 'moral support' mean? What does 'ameliorate their condition' mean? It made no sense!

While Babington thought about it. Pitt Taylor gravely said he thought it looked like Strutt was to go there and see what needed to be done to protect them.

Strutt had pulled out a cigarette and was trying to calm down. He was to go alone, by himself, into former enemy territory to see how the Habsburgs, could be made safer. Really, he hadn't realised he was such a capable fellow. He asked Babington if he knew why he had been chosen?

Babington suggested he might have been selected because he spoke German like a native and knew a lot of archdukes. Hadn't he spent considerable time in Austria before the war?

So did a lot of people, Strutt thought wrathfully. The world before the war seemed like several lifetimes ago. He thought of Florrie. They had planned to meet in Paris in two weeks time and then go on to St. Moritz.

Pitt Taylor put in a cheery thought. It could be that the situation at Eckartsau had already been ameliorated and Strutt's efforts might not be needed or wanted for that matter. He could return home straight away.

Strutt felt ill. Did they know nothing about the situation in Austria? He grimaced in resignation. He was a career soldier, an officer. What could he say?

He asked them if they had any idea where Eckartsau was? No they did not. Both Babington and Pitt Taylor were in sympathy with his plight, but could offer no suggestions how to proceed. They warmly shook his hand, gave him a Letter of Credit for expenses and wished him luck. Strutt stood, saluted and left them shaken. What was he supposed to do now? He went back to his room and sat on the bed to think about it, he would not allow it to become a nightmare. He would go to Eckartsau, see what was needed and report back to London. He needn't stay there long.

Where to begin? He decided to try the Navy first. They had maps. He would find out where Eckartsau was and how to get there. That afternoon he went over to Maghera on the mainland where the big ships docked and had a look round. Very shortly he found HMS *Lowestoft*, a dreadnought in dock for repairs and as luck would have it, he discovered it was in the hands of Commodore Kelly, a sandy-haired Naval Attaché he had known in Paris. Kelly looked at his maps and found Eckartsau was a tiny village on the Danube, north east of Vienna and close to the Hungarian border. Strutt asked if the *Lowestoft* might take him as far as Fiume? Kelly demurred, but said he could probably find him some other transport. Would Strutt mind doing him a favour in return?

Strutt, feeling himself overburdened already, was not receptive. What did he want exactly? It turned out Kelly had been landed with two men both in need of an escort. One was the naval officer in plain clothes who was on a secret mission to Vienna. The other was a King's Messenger en route for Belgrade. This didn't sound too onerous, so Strutt agreed.

The naval officer was called Lieutenant Paynter. He had brown hair and a beard to match. Strutt found him gaily helping himself from an excellent store of Navy cigarettes in the Lowestoft's canteen. Strutt decided this was not a bad idea and helped himself as well. He told the affable Paynter they could get acquainted later, he had things to do before they departed.

On the top deck, Commodore Kelly met him and told him suitable transport had been found to get him to Fiume. He was to be on board at 06.00 the following morning. Strutt was relieved that problem was solved. On leaving the *Lowestoft*, he paused on the quayside to look out over the harbour. Venice at this distance seemed like a city of the dead, surrounded by mines and floating batteries. How grey it looked. He was glad that he and Florrie had known it in happier times when the sunlight had danced in Piazza San Marco and the violins had played all day outside Café Florian. The Italians must have been in terror of losing the place.

Chapter Nine

February 24th 1919
Fiume Again

The next morning bright and early, he and his charges boarded HMS *Hydra*, a fine frigate which had been in the battle of Jutland. In command was a charming young man of twenty-two, Lieutenant Simpson. They got away at 6.45. The weather was dull and calm. They had to pass through minefields and shape a peculiar course along the coast right past the harbour of Pola, which was full of Italian battleships. These must be the ships, thought Strutt, whose commander was too cowardly to leave Brindisi and Taranto until after the Armistice was proclaimed. He'd heard all this as had everyone. Italian fighting skills were nowhere esteemed, which was a shame, because he knew that their soldiers were good fighters when properly led.

They arrived in torrents of rain at Fiume at 15.10 and tied up most skilfully at the quay. In the distance, other ships lay drunkenly against the quayside and the dock was lined with rusting iron cranes. Although he had just been here a few days ago, he felt the place had deteriorated in the interim. Of course he had not seen much of it last week.

On the main deck, Paynter was trying to help the King's Messenger, a twenty-three year old, late of the Scots Guards, called Childers. This young man had been shot in the stomach and lungs and discharged from the Army as totally unfit, and yet here he was by the folly of the Foreign Office, bringing out alone, with no one to help him, twenty heavy bags each as much as a man could handle.

Childers, of course, was dead keen and saw no problems. He told them the Foreign Office had issued him with a Red passport which would ensure all help along the way. Strutt sighed and emitted a few expletives into the uncaring air. It was quite clear Childers would not be able to leave Fiume, indeed depart this very spot, without help, so Strutt proceeded to get some.

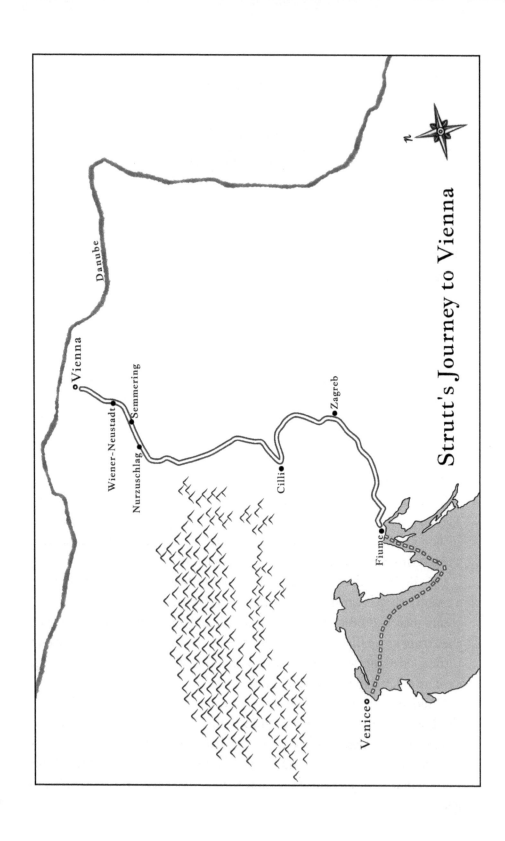

Strutt's Journey to Vienna

By the kindness of the Adjutant, 8th York and Lancaster Regiment stationed at Fiume, he secured the services of a regimental policeman, Lance Corporal Ashmore – a typical army conscript youth with slicked-down brown hair and a cheeky grin which showed his broken teeth to admiration. Strutt was not hopeful, but Ashmore proved to be very useful indeed.

He immediately took himself off to the railway station and found a porter with a large mail cart. He then bribed the porter to roll his cart all the way down to the quayside which was about a quarter of a mile. They all then helped Childers get his twenty grey canvas mail bags onto the cart, up to the railway station and onto the Zagreb train. There was a lot of heavy shoving, but they managed it. Strutt was not pleased by their success. He was staring at the train.

The train looked like it had taken a direct hit from a bomb earlier in the week. The old style First Class carriage had three compartments with no glass in the windows, no cushions and water trickled down through a vanished light fitting. What upholstery that was left was filthy. All the comforts of home, in fact, thought Strutt sardonically. This new job of his was not starting off well.

Next to him Paynter was muttering about how they were expected to travel on this. At this point, a shabbily uniformed conductor came up to them apologetically and seeing their shock, informed them that this train was in much better shape than the previous one, so they might count their blessings. 'Thank you', said Strutt not looking at the man. 'It is a great comfort to know we have the best there is. I expect the dining car was bombed as well? The lavatories?' The conductor shrank from the cold look in Strutt's eyes. He assured him the dining car was mostly in service and the facilities were undamaged. He then turned and scuttled off. Strutt's morose glance followed him down the platform. Where was the comfortable train he had travelled in last week?

Once aboard the train, Paynter kindly suggested Childers have the dryish inside seat. He could see the young man was about played out. Thanking him, Childers wrapped himself up as warmly as he could and fell asleep instantly. Ashmore got up into the guard's seat which was sticking up into the roof and was the only one to stay dry. That left Strutt with his choice of damp seats. He was seriously annoyed. It was ice cold. His leg was not going to like it.

They had been told that the trip to Zagreb would take ten hours. Strutt wrapped himself in his greatcoat and put a jumper around his neck and head. Hoar frost slowly covered everything inside the windows; the floor was covered in wet snow. During the night, he fortified himself with brandy from his flask and managed to sleep fitfully. What a bloody night. As they approached Zagreb, Strutt woke and wondered if he could move. He felt frozen solid. At this point, Ashmore handed him a steaming cup of coffee and life returned to his limbs.

He asked Ashmore how Childers was. Did he survive the night? Ashmore told him that Paynter had sat next to him the whole night to keep the worst of the draught off him. He was fine, they both were.

Strutt rose and stretched his limbs. Time to get off this purgatory of a train and find a hotel, but first they had to get Childers sorted out. He let Ashmore carry his bags.

Strutt found a couple of Slovakian train officials and made sure Childers got the help he needed. Soon porters were lugging the twenty bags onto a luggage wagon, Strutt noticed the men were all very thin and raggedly dressed. The British blockade, he thought, has taken its toll. After the porters were directed towards the correct train for Belgrade half hidden in a cloud of steam from its engine, Strutt smiled gravely at Childers who was thanking him profusely for all his help. 'When you get to Belgrade, be sure to use the Red passport.' Paynter and Ashmore grinned behind him and waved goodbye to the brave young man.

After a hot bath and a good breakfast at a hotel in the town, Strutt felt more able to face the day. Everything seemed grey. There was not much bomb damage, but the shops looked poor and the people poorer. He was itching to get to their train early to make sure they would get the compartment he had reserved. He refused to suffer another night like the last. First they had to go to the Sud Bahn station in another part of the town where they would pick up the Trieste-Vienna train.

Paynter and Ashmore duly followed behind Strutt at the new station. They had so far found him cynical, but not unfriendly, but here his demeanour changed. An elderly and very polite conductor awaited them at their carriage door. Strutt was immediately querulous, like a very starched British aristocrat anticipating trouble. He hoped there would be no difficulties about the compartment they had reserved for their sole use. There wasn't. The very deferential conductor bowed them to a carriage which was more or less intact. Strutt was relieved. Ashmore immediately set about carefully stowing away their kit, which included five days rations for the three of them that Strutt had the forethought to request from Commodore Kelly two days before. They'd already broached it before Zagreb, but the rest was untouched.

The railway officials who strolled up and down the train corridor were all Austrian and as polite as before the war. Once the train got under way, Paynter, a decent, but untraveled fellow, produced some Austrian wine and declared 'Well now, this is more like it, don't you think? It looks like the worst is over.' Strutt accepted a glass and saluted Paynter. He hoped he was right, but he wouldn't bet on it.

When the guard came along to see their tickets, Strutt electrified both men by letting fly with a short burst of angry German that made the man quail and retreat. *Kist die hand, Excellenz*, he murmured apologetically. Strutt looked at his amazed friends. 'I have been here before,' was all he said by way of explanation.

They were all deep into their books later when after struggling slightly with the door, a very respectable-looking lady sidled into their compartment and asked Strutt if he would be so very kind as to pretend that all her hand luggage in the next compartment was his as officials would be searching the train at the next stop for food and valuables. Her lovely brown eyes beseeched him. Nothing fazed, Strutt very politely refused and nearly had to lift her out of the compartment, something he did gently but firmly. Again, his companions were incredulous. Paynter even went so far as to exhibit his disapproval.

Strutt gave him a nasty look. What else was he to do? There would have been a fracas and they couldn't afford it at this stage. Paynter immediately shut up and looked out the window. Ashmore said nothing, but wondered why Strutt had asked him to stay on with him yesterday. He didn't seem to need anyone.

The next stop was across the border into Austria. All three men were dismayed when the snow abated for a moment as the train halted and starving children swarmed over the train windows. Little children with small narrow bones and big pleading eyes were perched on the shoulders of bigger children. They were all just bags of bones covered in rags. With little arms pounding on the windows they yelled 'bread, bread, please bread!' On the loud speaker, they heard a man shouting out that all must leave the train and be searched. Here was Strutt's companions' first experience of the starving population of Austria-Hungary. Stricken, the three men fumbled for their ration bags. A furiously frowning Strutt opened the window and the three of them doled out slices of British ration bread, the first white bread that many had seen in years. Ashmore reached for the tinned goods, but Strutt stopped him. This was only the beginning. All three were ashen-faced and Strutt was angry. Surely he had become inured to starving children by now, he thought. But it always hurt him at a deep level. Damn.

Ashmore was looking at his hands, visibly upset. Paynter stroked at his beard and tried to calm himself. He wanted to know if it was always like this or had some recent disaster caused it? Strutt was affronted at such ignorance. He turned on Paynter, and told him in a clipped voice that food shortages began in 1915 with the British blockade of the Adriatic. It was then that the Austrian government started hoarding food supplies for the army. The people came last. Did Paynter not know that most of Central Europe was starving? They had been starving for several years now. Thousands of children have died. Paynter replied faintly that he had been at sea until recently. He didn't know.

At this point, the conductor came along shouting 'Out, Out' to the passengers, but when he got to Strutt's compartment, he opened the door and quietly told him 'You will not be troubled, Excellenz.'

Ashmore was puzzled. What was going to happen now? He had clearly not understood the German lady's frantic plea for help when they began their journey in Zagreb. Why was everyone going to be searched? Were they looking for weapons? Strutt explained that what they were about to witness was robbery. The passengers were now going to be relieved of their foodstuffs and whatever other valuables the officials fancied. It was a very unfair and cruel world. Surely Ashmore had learned that by now?

It took a long while. Around them they could hear continuous shouting from the loud speaker, furious objections from the male passengers, screams from the women, and the pounding of slammed doors. Finally the train left the station in a cloud of smoke. The starving children were rounding on a new target – the officials.

They arrived at Steinbruck at 16.00 and went to find the next train for Vienna, which luckily was leaving shortly. Strutt descended on the Station Master and ordered him to clear a coupé for them. This was an end compartment with seats on one side only. It was more spacious than others. The man immediately complied. Soon an immensely long train headed by a gigantic rusty engine rumbled into the station belching dark smoke. They secured their four-seater coupe and Ashmore once again stowed their gear. By 16.30 they were again en route.

At Cilli, everyone but them was ordered from the train to be searched again. This time, instead of starving children, there were hundreds of small groups of grey, shapeless people huddled around small fires, some under the railway arches, others sheltering under makeshift tents. This was what was left of the city after heavy fighting. All the buildings they could see had been broken down for firewood. It was a scene from hell.

At Graz, there was a prolonged halt so that the same thing could happen again. This time, the officials claimed that German notes were not allowed to be taken into Austria. They were taking their money as well as their goods. Strutt and his party refused to dismount and the officials retired bowing. A fierce mien and a British uniform still count for something, by God, thought Strutt furiously. Young Ashmore, watching Strutt's display of arrogance, was developing a serious case of hero worship.

The same thing went on all night at every station, but the train ran well in the intervals and their coupe was mercifully free of vermin. Every now and then, when they travelled through towns, did they notice that nearly all the factories were closed. The only signs of life anywhere they could see were grey people diligently turning over the untilled fields for stray vegetables. Once they passed what looked like a great deserted ammunition works. Derelict guns and broken equipment lay strewn about.

With no more delays, the train arrived at the Sud Bahnof Station at Vienna at 12.10 the next day. Strutt considered it a successful, if unpleasant journey. Paynter and Ashmore found it harrowing and talked about it between themselves. Sleet was hurtling down from the sky. Outside the station, their luggage was put onto a cart drawn by two miserable, underfed horses. Strutt hated seeing that. Shortly, a car arrived to take them to the Hotel Bristol, where Strutt had often stayed in the past. Ashmore and Paynter followed him in.

Chapter Ten

February 27th, 1919
Vienna

The Hotel Bristol was one of the great hotels of the world and still lived up to its reputation. Its grand high-ceilinged reception hall was everything Strutt remembered. He relaxed. Naturally it was full, but the very civil manager, whom Strutt remembered, was persuaded into promising them rooms by 16.00. In the meantime, 'luncheon' or what passed for it would not be ready until 13.30, so Strutt decided to take a short walk around the Ring while Paynter telephoned various officials regarding his mission. Ashmore was left to keep an eye on their luggage.

Outside the weather was clear and someone had shovelled away the snow in front of the hotel. Strutt took a deep breath and gazed around him. Across the road was the famous park called the Ring, around which in former decades the nobility used to circle in their smart carriages at the fashionable hour. He remembered it well. The trees were looking bedraggled, but everything else was covered by a pretty veil of snow. He was musing there, when suddenly a figure loomed up in front of him and stopped. It was Kary Czernin, a dear old friend. They both stared at each other and burst into laughter.

'Bill, how wonderful to see you,' cried Czernin shaking his hand warmly. 'I thought you must be killed by now.' He was genuinely delighted to see him.

'They tried, Kary, they tried,' smiled Strutt. 'I seem to be harder to do away with than most.'

Czernin quickly asked him if he had lunched? He hadn't. He then invited him to come home with him immediately and have some. Maritschy, his wife, would be thrilled to see him. He then paused in confusion. There was a problem. He had just remembered they had nothing to eat! He looked comically flummoxed.

Strutt laughed at him. Food was not a problem. Leave it to him. He was shocked and happy to see Czernin again. He dashed back to the car and helped himself to their remaining loaves of bread and some tins of bully beef and jam and followed Czernin back to his enormous apartment in Schwarzenberg Platz, just around the corner from the Bristol. The same butler whom Strutt had known for years opened the door and took their coats and Strutt's parcels. Czernin then hurried him up the stairs and threw open the door of a cosy sitting room. 'Look what I found on the doorstep!', he announced to a figure curled up in a deep chair near the window. Countess Czernin, neé Maritschy Kinsky, looked up curiously. When she saw the figure in the door, she rose, one hand on her breast and cried 'Bill!' in a melodious voice. She couldn't believe it was really him. She flew across the room and hugged him. How wonderful it was to see him.

Czernin laughed, delighted at his wife's surprise. What had he told her?

Strutt, too, was so overwhelmed by the welcome that he forgot himself and hugged Maritschy back in front of Kary. No one had called him 'Bill' in a very long time. It was a name he associated with close friends, cosy fires and endless days and nights of companionable fun.

Maritschy was as charming as ever. Her eyes sparkled and her beautiful blond hair was caught up as usual in a chic bun, but she appeared thinner and careworn. Kary, too, was thinner than he remembered. The three friends hunkered down by the fire and Maritschy sent for a tray and plates after marvelling at the tins of bully beef. 'You see what we have come down to, Bill, but don't worry. It's not as bad as all that.' She flashed him her mischievous smile of old.

At a stroke, Strutt's cares fell away and he remembered the years of fun he and Florrie had had with Kary and Maritschy and their friends. They in turn, found him as he used to be – charming and full of humour, but older. There was so much to catch up on.

Over a picnic lunch in front of the fire, Kary asked Strutt what had brought him to Vienna? Strutt finished the last bite of his sandwich and told them he had come to see the Head of the British Military Mission on important business. Did he know him? The answer was yes. Kary quickly informed him that Colonel Cuninghame was right now at the British Embassy. He had seen him that morning, but he would not be there for long as he was in charge of both Vienna and Prague and, in fact, spent more time in Prague. If he wanted to see him, he should go immediately.

Strutt very reluctantly realised Kary was probably right and so, finishing his glass of wine, he tore himself away from the cosy scene, promising to return soon.

Count Ottokar von Czernin had enjoyed a spectacular career which by 1919 had fallen under a severe cloud. Born into an ancient Bohemian family in 1872, he had joined the Austro-Hungarian Foreign Service in 1895. By 1903, he was a member of the Bohemian Lower House and quickly made his name as a defender of 'monarchist principles,' which meant in practice that he opposed universal suffrage and rule by Parliament.

When war came in 1914, Czernin successfully managed to keep Romania neutral until 1916, when Romania trimmed its sails and joined the Allies. After that Czernin was appointed Minister of Foreign Affairs. The war was not going well. He, and his predecessors, had to face the horrible reality that if the war did not end soon, the Habsburg empire might collapse.

There followed numerous efforts to persuade Germany to end the war. In February 1918, Czernin signed a peace treaty with the newly created Ukrainian People's Republic. In March, he reached the highlight of his career by signing peace treaties with Russia and Romania. He was now ostensibly the leading diplomat of the Central Powers, but this was misleading. He was secretly being undermined by the new Emperor Karl who was making his own bid for peace with the Allies. This later became known as the notorious 'Sixtus Affair'.

What basically happened was this. In 1917, with war waging on all sides, the newly installed Emperor Karl, who was desperate to end the war, decided to secretly enter into peace negotiations with the French without the knowledge of his German allies. His motive was not to sideline his allies, but to take the initiative in seeking peace. Using his brother-on-law, Prince Sixtus of Bourbon-Parma as postman, he wrote a letter to Prime Minister Clemenceau, suggesting, among other things, that Germany might make certain territorial concessions to the French in order to secure peace. Nothing came of this effort.

Then in April 1918, Czernin, now Austria's Foreign Minister, gave a very aggressive speech to the Vienna City Council that was intended to strengthen fighting spirit and boost loyalty to Austria's ally in Berlin. In this speech, to emphasise the weakness of the Western Powers, he mentioned that France had made contact with Austria the year before looking to make a separate peace, but her demands were too unreasonable to be acceptable. He thus inferred that Clemenceau was the main obstacle of peace.

Prime Minister Clemenceau was incensed at this blatant falsehood and reacted cleverly. Instead of issuing loud denials to all and sundry, he told the press all about the Emperor's secret peace initiative, even going so far as to publish his letter. Thus the full story of the Emperor's betrayal of the Central Powers was there for all to read and a neat wedge was driven into the alliance between Germany and Austro-Hungary.

To make matters worse, Czernin claimed he had known nothing about the Emperor's peace initiative – which was untrue, though he might not have known the whole story. He then persuaded Karl to write a mendacious letter to the Germans saying he had never authorised Prince Sixtus' approach to the French. Karl wrote:

Monsieur Clemenceau's accusations against me are so base that I am not of a mind to discuss the matter with France any further. Henceforth our answer shall be our cannons in the west.

Unfortunately, his letter crossed with the publication of the other letter. It was horribly embarrassing and Czernin was forced to resign. Karl later discovered that Czernin had been in contact with the German Embassy throughout the crisis and had planned to persuade Karl to step down as Emperor because of the affair. It was a mad scheme, fraught with misunderstandings, jealousies, confused motives and malice.

Czernin seemed to have moved, in this increasingly confused muddle, from being loyal to his Emperor to thinking of the greater good of German hegemony over Austria. He had some idea of instigating a regency interlude to achieve, under his guidance, full union with Germany. After that Karl might be reinstalled on the throne as a puppet. Above, all Czernin was thrashing about trying hard not to be caught out as disloyal to either side – and that truly might have been his real position. It is possible he might have regarded Austria's alliance with Germany as so sacred, he was even prepared to sacrifice his monarch on its altar. At worst, it is also possible, that he was a megalomaniac and a traitor. Historians have not decided, but they do agree that the whole affair was a complete catastrophe for Austria.

The result was that a great bitterness descended on all concerned and Czernin, feeling the great chill from the Palace, lived in dread that he would be expelled from the Order of the Golden Fleece, which had been bestowed upon him only the year before. This order was the most prestigious and exclusive order of chivalry in the world. It was established in 1430 by Philip the Good, Duke of Burgundy and subsequently fell by inheritance to both the Bourbon Kings of Spain and Archdukes of Austria, who are its Grand Masters. To be admitted to the Golden Fleece was a tremendous honour, enormously coveted.

In the end, Strutt's feeling about the Sixtus Affair was that almost certainly both the Emperor and Czernin had been acting in good faith, but at cross purposes. Therefore both were equally at fault in the disaster, but of course, he could not say so.

Chapter Eleven

February 27, 1919
Cuninghame

Strutt walked to the British Embassy which was just on the other side of the Ring. Thankfully, someone had cleared the ice on the path. There he found Lieutenant Colonel Sir Thomas Cuninghame in his office buried under a pile of paperwork. The door was open and for a moment, he could watch Cuninghame unobserved. He recogised him immediately.

They had never formally met, but Strutt remembered him as the shifty-eyed fellow who had been a worthless Military Attaché at Athens in 1916; the Colonel who was always beautifully dressed, shining buttons and all. Someone had whispered into his ear to warn him. Cuninghame liked to pretend he was a bit of a fool, but he wasn't.

On seeing Strutt enter his office, Cuninghame stood and welcomed him with great affability spun with just a shade of condescension. Strutt's uniform was not at its best and he realised from Cuninghame's pursed glance that he cared about such things. He sat down before being offered a seat just to irritate the man. Cuninghame paused and returned to his seat behind the desk. Clearly this was not to be a social call.

Lieutenant Colonel Thomas Cuninghame was a tall, slender man of forty-two with a high forehead topped by thin brown hair. He had pale blue eyes and a thick moustache resting on his upper lip. He held himself proudly and looked the part of the efficient brave officer that he had once been. Sadly, his luck had run out early in his career. He had been in the thick of battle outside Ladysmith in South Africa in 1900, when a shell had burst near his legs and hurt him very badly. He was patched up as well as possible, but his fighting days were over much to his fury and disappointment. He was awarded the Distinguished Service Order (DSO).

After he recovered, he was posted to Pretoria to work in Intelligence. There his health collapsed again when he contracted typhoid fever. This time, the Army sent him back to England to recuperate. In 1906, while riding near Bagshot, he was thrown by his horse and fractured his skull. He was devastated.

In 1907, after he recovered, he was sent out to Ireland to work for the 1st Rifle Brigade's Quartermaster General. He had taken his wife of three years standing and the first of their two children with him. He was not happy working in a backwater and not terribly happy with his marriage either,[1] but they remained in Ireland for five long years. He had felt marooned.

In 1912, after much string pulling, he managed to secure an appointment as Military Attaché in Vienna. He was thrilled. His task was to gather Intelligence from over the whole of the Austro-Hungarian Empire, Greece and Russia. He was delighted to be in the great world again. In 1914 they sent him to Athens to help the British Minister get the Greeks on the Allied side.

Finally in 1919, he was sent back to Austria to become the Military Attaché between Vienna and Prague. Many would say, Cuninghame had had a very successful career, but not he. He had wanted to be known for his fighting prowess and his leadership in battle. Instead, he had been forced to make do with desk jobs which he considered beneath his abilities.

Strutt kicked off their discussion by expressing himself glad to have caught Cuninghame in Vienna. There was a delicate matter on which he wished to ask his opinion. He told Cuninghame about his orders and watched the play of emotions cross the man's face.

Of course, Cuninghame knew all about Strutt's mission. In his private opinion, it was a quixotic task that would almost certainly blow up in Strutt's face and cause maximum embarrassment in London. On the other hand, he coveted the job for himself. He had known from Intelligence received, that all was not well with the Imperial Family, but it had nothing to do with him. Then he received orders to send out a doctor to Eckartsau to see what was needed. He did so. He sent Dr Summerhayes. He was then ordered to go there himself to report from a military viewpoint. He was elated. Then, on the heels of the first message another one arrived

---

1. They were divorced in 1925.

telling him very firmly to stay away from Eckartsau. Someone else was being dispatched to deal with the Imperial Family.

Cuninghame had been both annoyed and offended. Here was an unlikely chance for glory with fascinating people and he was being not just overlooked, but actively ordered to stand down. Well, Strutt was bound to fail in any case, but out of curiosity and prudence, he thought he might unofficially enquire about Strutt's record. He still had friends in Intelligence.

After listening to everything Strutt had to say, Cuninghame casually revealed he'd recieved a message about it a couple of days before and had sent out Dr Summerhayes from the Royal Medical Corps, attached to the British Food Commission to see if he could be of use. He assured Strutt that everyone at Eckartsau was healthy enough. All seemed in hand there, according to the good doctor. Of course, Summerhayes did not have Strutt's expertise in warfare, so he couldn't make a military assessment. Cuninghame eyed Strutt benignly.

He then proceeded to enumerate some of the difficulties Strutt would no doubt encounter. The most pressing of these was the problem of the Imperial Couple's continuing safety. Dr Summerhayes had reported he had not seen many soldiers on guard at the castle. If their situation became dangerous or the current provisional government decided to detain the Emperor, on whatever pretext, Strutt could be faced with having to get the Imperial Family out of Austria altogether. At the horrified look on Strutt's face when he said this, Cuninghame almost grinned.

'What?!' said Strutt taken aback. Those were not his orders. He was there to give moral support and ameliorate any difficulties, nothing that could not be done in a few days.

Cuninghame pursed his lips. Of course, that is what they would tell him, but the problem on the ground was quite different. He viewed his nails for a moment and then smiling, he leaned across his desk to inform Strutt that his real job here was to keep the Imperial Family alive and safe.

Strutt was appalled and got up and walked to the window. This was a nightmare. Just how was he supposed to do that and for what purpose? Who cared about the Habsburgs, anyhow? He couldn't get his head around it. He turned and asked Cuninghame if he had any idea why he had been specifically chosen for this outrageous mission. He had never even met the Emperor.

Cuninghame, sitting comfortably back in his chair, was smugly pleased and did not mind showing it. He knew Strutt's background now, his outstanding war record. He knew how his sometimes unorthodox, hands-on-skills and command of languages had often made a huge difference to the success of a campaign – and heartily disliked him for it. This job might have been his! He pulled a cigarette from his case and lit it. Through the resultant smoke ring, Cuninghame opined that perhaps he was chosen because somewhere on his very illustrious Catholic family tree dangled a knight errant. He smiled maliciously at the mental picture.

Strutt eyed him with contempt. 'Preferably by the neck, I'm sure', he replied.

Strutt was puzzled. What had his family got to do with anything? Cuninghame's knowledge of his family must be sparse, Strutt thought, but that seemed to be enough to bring forth an ugly, uncalled for jealousy. What a rotter the man was. Yes, Strutt's grandfather was the first Lord Belper, a wealthy industrialist, and former Chancellor of the Duchy of Lancaster, but he himself was the offspring of a younger son. It was on his mother's side, that he had more claim to gentility. The March Philipps de Lisles were an old Leicestershire family who had married well. It was her father who had become a Catholic convert and raised his family in that religion.

Cuninghame laughed. He was going to enjoy the story as it unfolded. He rose from his chair and invited Strutt to come and meet the rest of the staff. He would be dealing with them more than with himself. Cuninghame was in Prague most of the time.

In the outer office, Strutt was introduced to Phillpots, a middle-aged non-entity with wispy hair and spectacles. Phillpots, he would come to appreciate was very reliable. Then there was 'old' Eisenmann, who had been a kind of secretary there for twenty-five years and more. He looked a decent enough fellow, but he was an Austrian and secret British documents passed through his hands. Strutt smiled wryly. How like the Foreign Office, he thought. Wonderful. Our very own resident spy.

A disabled officer, Nicholson, completed the staff. He would be dealing mainly with Phillpots and, of course, old Eisenmann. Strutt suggested to Cuninghame that they continue their discussion over lunch at the Bristol. There was a lot more he needed to know.

They left the embassy and walked into the busy, tree-lined avenue. The city seemed to be well on its way to finding its feet again. Several cars went by and a few horse-drawn drays. Snow had been shovelled to the side of the pavement and salt had been thrown down. The air was cold and clean. A few people, like themselves bent upon their business, strode about. Shortly, they came to the German Embassy. Cuninghame told him to ignore the Hun officials staring insolently down upon them from the large French windows on the first floor. Strutt had no trouble doing just that.

At the Bristol, they found there was practically nothing to eat for lunch, but Cuninghame produced a bottle of some excellent French burgundy, which the head waiter had kept for him. Ashmond Bartlett, the inquisitive Daily Telegraph correspondent, sat down at their table and was as objectionable as ever. Lt Paynter joined them for a while, and then went over to another table to talk to Countess Hoyos (*née* Whitehead) on some business. After the meal which consisted of one lone Viennese sausage and fried onions on toast, Strutt excused himself and went to telephone Colonel Summerhayes, who was still at Eckartsau, to arrange a car to be sent to fetch him the following day. Cuninghame had departed before he returned to the table. Strutt was unconcerned, as he had already taken the man's measure.

Chapter Twelve

February 27, 1919
At the Czernins

Strutt left the Bristol, his brain churning. For Cuninghame to tell him that he alone was now responsible for keeping the Emperor and Empress of Austria alive and well, was just bizarre. What had he got into? He had no clear idea. He decided to keep quiet about it until he had more information.

Within a few minutes he was back at the Czernin house where he ran into Maggie, the eldest daughter, on the stairs. He was amazed. She was grown up. The last time he saw her she was twelve and now he was astonished to see her grown tall and pretty in a forest green wool frock. Where did the years go, he wondered. He bowed and complimented her on managing to grow up to be so lovely, which made Maggie blush and smile. She shyly welcomed him back.

Upstairs in the drawing room, Kary and Maritschy were waiting for him. It was time for him to be brought up to date on the situation in Austria. Kary looked worn and worried, his nerves were obviously badly strained. Strutt thought he looked sixty rather than forty-four and had to restrain himself from remembering former times. He got straight down to business and asked him what the general feeling was about the Emperor and Empress. Kary replied 'No man, woman or child desires their return to the throne now. They are finished.' He was scathing about the Empress as well. People knew before that the Emperor was weak, but they loved him. Now they see him as the weak dupe of a strong-willed troublemaker – his wife and a foreigner to boot. The mess they made of trying to sue for peace behind the Germans' backs was a disaster for them. They were calling it The Sixtus Affair after her meddling brother.

Strutt, sipping a light drink, said he had heard something about it.

'Yes,' replied Czernin, 'but, I warrant not all of it.' He sat down opposite Strutt and explained. For a while there, it looked like the Emperor might succeed in his negotiations with the French. He and the Foreign Ministry, were impressed and surprised, but then the Italian Foreign Minister, Sonnino, got to hear of it. As Strutt must know, the Italians were expecting to annex some territory from Austria after the war and indeed, Sonnino had convinced himself that the Allies had promised this to him. Then to his fury, in discussions with the French Foreign Minister one day, Sonnino caught a whiff that Austria was not going to keep her promise.

Sonnino was angry, but he contained himself until a few weeks later, thinking to curry favour with the Germans who might still win the war, Sonnino told the Germans the whole story! This was news to Strutt, but he said nothing. He noticed that Czernin did not mention his disastrous speech to the Viennese City Council.

Maritschy leaned forward and offered Strutt some olives. Her eyes said this was a story she had heard many times.

Czernin rose to his feet and started walking around. Well, he was sure Strutt could imagine what happened after that. The Germans were outraged that their 'weakling' ally should impertinently try to sue for peace behind their back and the result was they marched into Austria and took over what remained of the Imperial army.

Kary sat down again and put a hand to his brow. Maritschy reached for his other hand and tried to calm him down.

Strutt realised this was very grave. He had heard all sorts of stories about the famous Sixtus Affair, not all of them consistent. Czernin clearly didn't want to admit he had a hand in the whole thing, so Strutt suggested the mess was surely the fault of the Italian and French Foreign Ministers? Czernin could not think of blaming himself?

Maritschy answered for her husband who was silent. What did it matter now? It was clear the people didn't want the Habsburgs back. She looked down at her hands, and in a stricken voice told him a lot of people thought the Emperor was a liar, a deserter and a traitor to their so-called friends the Germans. As for the Empress, she was hated by all. The Germans call her 'the Frenchwoman', because they say she was ready to sacrifice German interests to further the interests of her Bourbon kinfolk and in Austria they call her 'the Italian' because of her Parma connections. That's what they are saying. Poor thing, she can't win no matter what she does. At this she smiled at him sadly.

Strutt was intrigued. He asked them what did they think really happened? The Emperor could not have been so foolish to think he could really affect peace on his own?

Maritschy thought the Emperor and his wife were just desperate to do something to stop the war. They were newly on the throne, and were young, optimistic. The country was suffering horribly. Who knows?

Kary, sitting on the sofa, meanwhile had gathered himself together. He gave Strutt a long perambulation about what should happen next, which made little sense to him. Kary ended by saying the reason starvation started in Austria in early 1915 was that Germany who started the war, was prepared for war. Austria wasn't. 'But we did everything we could!' With this plea for understanding, he walked out of the room.

Strutt asked Maritschy if he was all right. Maritschy sighed and went to refresh Strutt's drink from the drinks tray behind the sofa. She told him Kary was under great stress. He did blame himself for a lot of things. Strutt must forgive him. Most of their old friends didn't understand. Very few of them actually fought in the war, you see. It was rather shaming.

Strutt was not aware that most of the great Austro-Hungarian families had sat out the war and privately wondered if it were actually true. 'It's hard to believe they would not raise a hand to fight off the Boche – and you must forgive me for using that term.'

Maritschy sadly laughed and said the only thing she minded was when the French spoke about the 'sous-boches', meaning them, the Austrians! This expression was new to Strutt. He knew 'boche' was French slang for 'rascal', but during the war and later it came to have a connotation of the worst sort of beast.

She sat down again near him and her gay demeanour faded. Strutt was alarmed as her lovely grey eyes began to swim with unshed tears. 'Bill, things are not good here. They are very bad. Kary's life is in danger. I know it is.' She looked at him beseechingly. 'We have to get away.'

Strutt took her hand and told her she should always know that if he could help, he would. No question, but at the moment he was trying to find out exactly what his own situation was. It took a little time to quieten her immediate fears, but he did not grudge it. After doing his best to cheer her up, he left and returned to the Bristol. There was a lot to think about and tomorrow he would find out what he would be dealing with at Eckartsau. One thing was for sure, he was going to do the basic minimum and then get out. He was not going to get involved.

Chapter Thirteen

February 28, 1919
Eckartsau

The next morning, a huge open Daimler, bearing the Imperial crest, arrived to drive him and Ashmore to Eckartsau. Ashmore was proving quite invaluable as messenger and general assistant, and so Strutt had cleared it with the relevant authorities to keep him on.

The young military policeman, with his broken-tooth grin, had been stricken to silence on their harrowing rail journey from Zagreb to Vienna, but he had soon recovered. He was naturally curious, unreflective and generally seemed to think well of people. Strutt wondered how he ever came to be selected for his job in the police. The Military Police he had met were hardened men, not happy optimists.

Both men, while wrapping up well in the fur rugs supplied, ignored an old man who was speaking to the driver. He had walked away when they got into the car. Ashmore, of course, sat in front with the driver, leaving Strutt with his own thoughts on the seat behind. One of those immediate thoughts was that driving a car with the Imperial crest clearly visible was not the best idea. Surely the Emperor had more discretion than that? The man was either very brave or very foolish. Strutt was not pleased to start with and this just added another grief to his list.

They left the hotel at 10.00 and drove at a great pace through the town, over the long Reichsbrucke Bridge that spanned the icy Danube and on through Lebau to Aspern, where they passed the imposing Austrian Lion statue put up to commemorate an occasion about which Strutt wrote in his diary – 'when the Austrians came more near to winning a victory than usual.'

After Aspern the road became very bad especially beyond Orth. The driver stopped the car to put up the roof just as the rain started. After a while the rain turned to snow, and they were grateful for the rugs. The scenery was depressing in the extreme. Out in the frozen fields, he could

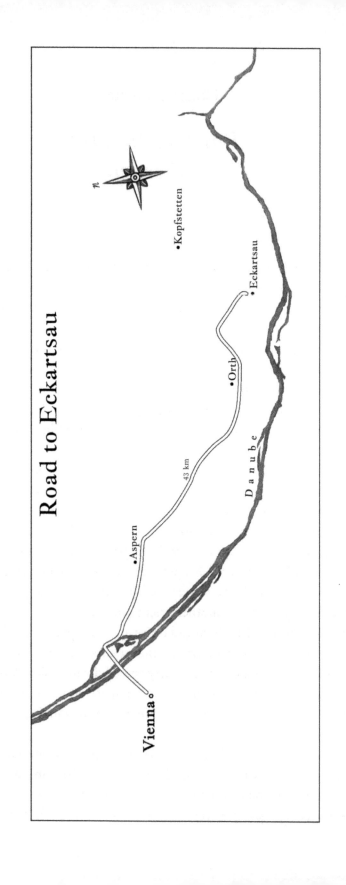

Road to Eckartsau

Vienna

•Aspern

43 km

D a n u b e

•Orth

•Eckartsau

•Kopfstetten

see snow-clad people searching for remnants of food. Strutt ruminated that it would take years to make the land productive again and from where would the work force come? Between 1870 and 1910, hundreds of thousands of people left the land for the cities. With so many of them now dead, who was left? He signed, remembering his visits to Austria before the war, how lovely it had all been. How bountiful. He stopped thinking.

Approaching the small village of Eckartsau and the vast woods surrounding it, the road became a morass through which the car thrashed and skidded its way out in second gear until they reached the entrance to the drive. A uniformed Austrian policeman and a fierce-looking canine were on duty. The policeman waved them through with a salute, he was expected.

The handsome tree-lined drive down to the castle was about a quarter of a mile long. As they made the final turn, Strutt saw an imposing two-storied building with two wings flanking an ornate central block with an arch, through which they drove into a large courtyard. The rain had stopped. It was 11.30am.

Strutt got out of the car and glanced around. The courtyard was not large, but appropriate to the size of the house. A few cars were parked to one side. It was all rather baroque. Strutt was annoyed that the 60-km drive had taken them nearly two hours, but he conceded the road had not been good. On a drier day, the going would be faster. So here he was. He steeled himself to greet the welcoming party.

Waiting to greet him were Dr Summerhayes, sent by the British Food Commission, Herr Schager, a paunchy States Councillor and Shonta von Seedak, a naval lieutenant with a neat, if slightly over large brown moustache and intelligent eyes. Inside the castle, Strutt was introduced to the Empress' two young ladies in waiting: the young Countesses Bellegarde and Schoenborn and also to Countess Bellegarde's fiancé, Count Joseph Hunyady, whom Strutt vaguely remembered meeting before. Hunyady was Steward to the Imperial Household and a close friend of the Emperor. It was all very cordial and proper. They were all thrilled to see him.

Strutt found the two ladies very attractive in different ways. Gabriella Bellegarde was slightly above average height for a woman, with lovely brown eyes set under well-arched brows in a wide oval face. Agnes

Schoenborn, on the other hand was petite with short wavy blond hair and a sweet smile. Both were the sort of intelligent and beautiful women he liked. Hunyady was older than they, probably in his early forties. He was tall, good-looking with fine dark eyes and he stood well. Strutt later discovered he had acted as mentor at one time to the Emperor and still had considerable influence. All three of them made favourable impressions on Strutt, but he had his eye on Shonta who looked the most attentive.

Hunyady took it upon himself to see Strutt to his room and was very chatty on the stairs. Very diplomatically, he asked Strutt if he had been to Eckartsau before. Strutt had not. Did he know that it had been Archduke Franz Ferdinand's favourite shooting lodge? Strutt smiled. 'He never mentioned it to me. I knew him well, as it happens, but mainly in St. Moritz. His Highness was a great skier, you know.' Hunyady did know this, but he wasn't a skier himself. Strutt was setting down a marker. He knew Hunyady would now take him seriously.

They finished climbing the long marble stairs which ran gracefully around two sides of the enormous reception hall. The baroque carvings and marvellous frescoed ceilings were very well done. The castle owed its baroque design to an eighteenth century royal chamberlain who had bought the original medieval fortress in 1720 on behalf of Emperor Franz I, husband of Maria Theresa. It was he who gave it the splendour which adorned the festive dinners and glittering balls of that time. His noble friends could also enjoy the shooting in the hunting grounds. The wild-life was undisturbed most of the year in this under-populated corner of the countryside.

They turned to go up another flight to find Strutt's room. It was a gorgeously appointed apartment with a bathroom attached. Strutt was delighted to be so comfortably accommodated and said so. Ashmore followed him into the room and began stowing the luggage. Count Hunyady then took his leave saying he would return in an hour to take him to see the Emperor.

Strutt looked around. The room was far more than agreeable. It was pre-war and everything in it from the luxurious four-poster bed with its silk coverings to the gilt mirrors and heavily curtained windows spoke of comfort. Strutt sighed. He could feel some of the tension he had been carrying fall way.

'Come over here, sir, and have a look at this.' Ashmore had spotted a photo of Strutt with Archduke Franz Ferdinand displayed on a collage screen. Strutt walked over to have a look. Sure enough, next to a photo of the Archduke and the young Kaiser of Germany in front of a small mountain of dead stags, Strutt perceived a photo of himself taken with the Archduke and his ADC Rumerskirch many years ago at St. Moritz. They were skiing.

Strutt was amused. He told Ashmore that he would find it hard to believe, but the Archduke had a photographer with him nearly all the time. To record his movements for posterity, he said. It was mad really, but it was one of the foibles his friends had to accept. A lot of people thought the Archduke was an evil man, but he wasn't really. He was certainly free with his opinions and unpopular because of them, but to his friends and especially to his family, he was extremely kind. Strutt had liked him, but he admitted he wasn't an easy man to know. Some people actually hated him. Ashmore suggested it must have been one of those who assassinated him.

Strutt smiled at this cheeky statement. Poor Sophie Chotek didn't deserve to die with her husband. Theirs had been a morganatic marriage, but a very happy one. The old Emperor Franz Joseph couldn't allow his nephew to marry so far beneath him. He thought it unseemly that a future Emperor would have a lowly baroness for a mother. It was a pity really. She was a nice woman and so were the children, what he had seen of them.

Ashmore asked what morganatic meant. He told him it meant that though they were legally married, their children could not inherit their father's position or titles. They would carry their mother's surname. In this case, as she had been created Duchess of Hohenberg, they would be Hohenbergs.

Strutt then remembered he had once asked Czernin what he thought would be the fate of the Archduke. The Count had told him he was quite sure the Archduke would be murdered one day by one of the legions of people whom he had insulted – and so he was and by a Serb, too. He was always particularly nasty about the Serbs.

While they were chatting, Ashmore was laying out Strutt's kit on the bed. Good God, what a state it was in! Strutt was overcome with shame. He told Ashmore to brush down his dress uniform immediately and get someone to do the laundry. He had better polish up the medals and his shoes as well. Hop to it. There wasn't much time.

Unknown to Strutt at this time, Zita had watched his arrival from her study window which looked out over the snowy courtyard. She, and her ladies in waiting, had been working all morning trying to locate more food. Normally, Gabriella worried about that and Agnes dealt with the family and household problems, but food had become an all absorbing difficulty. Zita was concerned about what would happen if Colonel Strutt couldn't help them.

The three of them watched the Colonel get out of his car. The snow was blowing through the leafless trees and falling on the baroque fountain in the castle courtyard. He looked very serious in his great coat as he shook hands with the welcoming party. Zita told her ladies they had better hurry down to greet him as well and they hurried out.

Left alone, she went to the fire. It was warm enough in the study, but that didn't stop the fear circling like an icy chill around her ankles. Three months ago when the Armistice was signed in November, she had persuaded Karl that they must flee to Eckartsau. She was frightened of what might happen to them at the hands of the mob if they stayed in Vienna. They both thought they would be safer here.

Now it was February and food was getting more difficult to obtain. How was she, the once all-powerful Empress of Austria-Hungary, going to continue to feed her children? Not to mention the entire Court now sleeping in reception rooms and passage ways? As always, they expected to be looked after. She couldn't let them down.

At the moment they were awaiting the food wagons which were overdue. She went to poke at the small fire in the grate. A few days ago, they had been delighted when Dr Summerhayes had suddenly appeared from the newly set up British Food Commission in Vienna. There were many small winter illnesses in the household and he had been very kind. Fortunately, the children had fully recovered from the influenza and the Emperor was nearly recovered from his heart attack. The Doctor had told her King George was sending someone to help them and now he was here.

She still couldn't understand why. If the French had refused them refuge despite their strong family links, why should the British give aid when they had every reason to hate them and there were no family links.

It was astonishing. She supposed it just showed the fair-mindedness of the British, especially if their King understood that they had tried to stop the war. On the other hand, perhaps she wasn't giving Sixtus enough credit for his powers of persuasion.

Yesterday, Joseph Hunyady had come joyfully into her office waving a telegram to say that a Lt Colonel Edward Strutt would shortly arrive. All the message said was that he had an outstanding war record, spoke several languages including German; he was a Catholic and was arriving from the Eastern Front. That was all. No more details. Zita had sent up a prayer for deliverance. Joseph had said Strutt should be interesting, if nothing else. That Front had been such a mess they had lost track trying to make sense of it.

But what could one man do, she had asked him. What could just one man do for them?

Chapter Fourteen

February 28, 1919
Meeting the Emperor and Empress

Less than an hour later, Count Hunyady came for him and Strutt, now washed, shaved and dressed as smartly as possible in the circumstances, was taken down to the Emperor's apartment and presented.

Strutt knew little about Karl von Habsburg, except that he was thirty-one years old and had tried to stop the war in 1916 when he succeeded to the throne. The resultant catastrophe of the Sixtus Affair was mainly his fault, but perhaps not entirely, in Strutt's opinion. He had meant well. Strutt was expecting to meet a well-set up young man of some intelligence.

He did not expect, when he entered the simply furnished room, to find the Emperor standing at attention saluting him, wearing what appeared to be his father's clothes. The pale blue uniform of a Field Marshal complete with sword, medals and 'plaques' hung on his slightly-built, frail figure swaying in front of the fire. Strutt's eyes involuntarily widened in surprise as he automatically returned the salute.

'Your Imperial Majesty,' he said eyes front.

Good God, what was this? In a burst of boyish confidence and a big smile, the Emperor told him that his finery was to honour King George who had very kindly come to his aid. 'We are so grateful', he said diffidently. 'We thank God you have come.' Strutt was immediately warmed by the Emperor's charm, but concerned that he might keel over at any minute.

'May we sit down, Sir? You do not look entirely well.'

'Everybody fusses. I am quite well', replied the Emperor waving his hand. 'I had a very slight heart attack a few months ago, but I am over it.' He unbuckled his heavy sword and placed it beside his chair.

Strutt looked again at the Emperor's thin features. He was quite handsome and well-bred, but the face lacked strength. 'I am very glad to hear it, Sir,' he said trying to put some confidence into his voice.

Automatically, he had registered three of the medals the Emperor was wearing – the Iron Cross, the Golden Fleece and the British Knight Grand Cross of the Victorian Order! The Emperor could not always have been as frail as he was now. He was intrigued.

The Emperor offered him a cigarette and gaily began to tell him how Dr Summerhayes arrived two days before and became a God-send to his people in the castle. All their ailments, real and imagined, got an airing. They briefly discussed the political situation and Karl assured him that they were safe at Eckartsau.

He told Strutt that he and the Empress had chosen Eckartsau as a refuge because of the loyalty of the people there. This was not Crown Land, he explained. This land was part of the Habsburg private heartland, indisputably his. Karl was confident that his throne was not yet lost and that the country would stabilise soon in his favour. Strutt said nothing. In any case, said the Emperor, there was nothing to worry about for the moment.

He rose from his chair and moved about. Of course, they would talk in more depth that evening. Now he urged Strutt to have lunch, and afterwards he had asked Lt Von Seedak to show him around. He pressed a button on his desk and Shonta entered. The Emperor then, very seriously, shook Strutt's hand firmly and stated again how genuinely grateful he was that Strutt had come. There was such sincerity in his young eyes, Strutt couldn't help but be a little moved, 'Oh, I nearly forgot,' he said as Strutt walked out the door. 'I believe the Empress has expressed a wish to see you at tea. You will be called.'

In his diary a few days later, after getting to know the Emperor better, Strutt wrote that the Emperor's appearance was deceptive. Yes, he was physically and mentally weak, but he was not a fool either. He had commanded troops in his younger days and he was ready to face his end like any other soldier. You had to respect his bravery in the face of his health and his situation. He did not complain. His endless charm made him intensely lovable as well. The whole persona could be confusing. One surprised Austrian general had described him thus: 'You hope to meet a thirty year-old, but you find a man with the appearance of a twenty year-old who thinks, speaks and acts like a ten year-old.' This was quite unfair, Strutt wrote, 'but sadly it seems to be not an uncommon opinion.'

Lt Von Seedak showed Strutt the way down to the large castle dining room. The noise was considerable. Four magnificent crystal chandeliers hung from the painted and gilded ceiling. Long portraits of royal personages interspersed the walls between carved panelling and marble statues. The whole effect was lavish, but restrained. This was a shooting lodge, not a palace, although one might be forgiven for thinking so considering the exuberant baroque entrance hall. Four long tables filled the room. Strutt figured there were at least sixty people present, but that wouldn't account for children and servants, he thought. Just how many people were living here, he wondered. It might matter.

Shonta found them seats at one of the long tables, telling him that their Majesties prefer to lunch alone with one or two advisers. It could get a bit noisy in here and the Emperor still tired easily. Strutt immediately picked him up on this. He told Shonta he could see that His Majesty had not yet recovered his health and boldly asked him what the doctors had to say about it. This was an impertinent question on such short acquaintance, especially to an underling, but Strutt had a growing feeling he needed to know everything about the current situation as soon as possible.

Shonta, stroked his silky, full moustache and told him the doctors were pleased with the Emperor's recovery so far, but that it would take more time for him to fully regain his strength. They were all confident that he would. His smile was bright.

They sat down and plates were served to them which contained very little food. The menu consisted of a thin vegetable soup, fried bean cutlets and dry biscuits. All this was served on magnificent Imperial china with elaborate silver and crystal adornments scattered down the heavy damask tablecloth. Strutt was unimpressed. At least the coffee was to his taste.

Shonta introduced him to Count Alexander Esterhazy who was seated next to him. He was one of the Emperor's two chamberlains. Strutt knew the name, of course, but had never met him. Esterhazy was one of the Hungarian magnates who were the true rulers of Hungary. Holders of vast inherited estates, these immensely wealthy noblemen made it very difficult for the official government to get anything done. (This situation extended more or less unchanged until the Second World War, when Hungary was overrun by the Red Army in 1944-45.). He greeted him formally.

Then to Strutt's embarrassed surprise, Esterhazy presented the man sitting directly across the table. It was the man who had been speaking to Strutt's driver just prior to his departure from Vienna. He turned out to be Colonel Count Ledohoffski, the Emperor's senior chamberlain. Strutt was mortified to discover that this very unassuming, gentle creature, had been asking his chauffeur if there was room in the car for him. Unfortunately, neither he nor his chauffeur had dared to ask Strutt! Later on, all three men became great friends. Esterhazy had all the charm of his countrymen and Ledo, who was a very sweet fellow, but terrified of any responsibility, amused the rest of them with his encyclopaedic knowledge of ancient Court scandal.

Strutt's other table companions greeted him very cordially. They were eager to hear the latest news from Vienna. He obliged by answering what questions he could. The major subject of conversation appeared to be the Bolshevik menace, everyone had an opinion. After leaving the dining room, Strutt grasped Shonta's elbow and nudged him into a window embrasure. In a low voice he asked him what danger he thought the Bolsheviks presented to them here.

Shonta snorted. Strutt might well ask. For weeks the Bosheviks and other filthy insurgents had been causing trouble in the neighbouring towns not fifteen miles away, but so far they have kept away from them. Strutt did not like the sound of this. Fifteen miles was not that far away. He told Shonta that they should meet again in twenty minutes at the front entrance. It was time they discovered just how safe they were at Eckartsau. He nodded at Ashmore who had finished his own lunch at another table and come out to join him.

Twenty minutes later, the three men, warmly and more casually dressed, met at the front entrance and proceeded to walk around the perimeter of the castle, which was of a decent size with three large wings protruding from the rear. There was not a garden as such, but a park laid out with attractive ornamental trees and a few benches. Straight in front of them, about half a mile away, they could just make out the Danube. To the right and left, the view was framed by trees. It was an attractive scene, but bleak at this time of year. He remembered that the court would only have come here in the shooting season, so a garden filled with flowers wasn't needed.

The three men gave careful attention to what defences had been built in to protect the house from marauders. What they discovered did not make Strutt happy. The medieval fortress had been comprehensively demolished to create a castle which was nothing more than a large mansion with strong wooden shutters on the ground floor, nothing else. A few men could breach the house in a matter of minutes.

He idly asked Shonta how many men their Majesties had brought with them for protection and was brought up sharp when he saw Shonta was embarrassed. What was this? Shonta looked down as he told him he was sorry to say they had only ten reliable Austrian police officers with them and worse, these police officers were the sole representatives of law and order in the whole country.

Strutt was shocked. My God, had the Emperor not brought at least a brigade of soldiers with him for protection? It seemed not. Shonta defended them. Their Majesties didn't think they would need protecting. All the people were loyal here and had been for six hundred years. Three months ago, Eckartsau was safe, the safest place in the whole country for them. Strutt had heard this before and told Shonta grimly that while this may have been true in November, he didn't believe it was true now.

They all walked on through the leafless trees towards the Danube. Along the way they saw several stags feeding in the sodden and depressed-looking clearings. Shonta told him that owing to poachers, there were only about two hundred deer remaining out of a thousand before the war.

The Danube was about two hundred yards wide and very swift when they got to it. Deep rocky embankments extended all the way from Vienna to Pressberg on each side. It was a sunny day, but cold as usual. The river was still carrying great clumps of ice, but there weren't so many now and the water was freely flowing. At least, thought Strutt, there is nowhere handy for any insurgents to land safely.

In the late afternoon, after he had washed and changed again to his well-brushed dress uniform, Strutt was summoned from his room to have tea with the Empress. So far, he did not see what he could possibly do to 'ameliorate' anyone's condition here. He was still very angry at having been put in this position. Here were at least a hundred vulnerable people, utterly defenceless and they were all somehow counting on him to save them. It was impossible, unsupportable. He was going to ask to be relieved. It would take a small army to get them out of here and even if that were managed, where could they safely go? He felt a little sorry for the frail Emperor, but after all, he got himself into this.

As he followed a footman down the stairs and along the cold, unlit main corridor leading to the Empress' private sitting room, he was in a foul mood. They duly arrived at her door and the footman knocked. After a moment, a smiling, but silent, Countess Bellegarde opened it and invited him in. The fully panelled room was warm with a cosy fire. The heavy curtains were drawn and a lamp brightened the tea table. Strutt glanced quickly around the room and saw three desks in shadow by the windows. At a right angle next to the fire a green velvet sofa sat with some sort of red and gold rug thrown over. A low table and two easy chairs faced it.

The Empress Zita gracefully rose from the sofa and he bowed to her. She was simply dressed in black and he noticed she was wearing wonderful pearls, a long rope thrown twice around her neck. She looked a bit pale and ill to him, but it might have been the lack of light. She was smaller than the average woman of her time, slightly built and looked younger than her twenty-six years, but all that was misleading. Strutt's first impression told him he was in the presence of a woman of considerable strength of character. He could feel it radiating from her like a tangible force. He blinked. Here was a true Queen, he thought. Determination was written in the lines of her firm chin and intelligence lit the vivacious brown eyes gleaming under her broad forehead half hidden by masses of dark hair. She was not a great beauty but with her soft, disarming charm and the rest, he was quite simply bowled over.

He struggled not to show it, but of course, she did notice and tactfully turned away for a moment to give him time to compose himself before expressing her gratitude for his arrival. She gestured to the arm chair opposite and he sat down. In the most charming manner, she enquired if his room lacked anything he needed and then about his journey. She was practical, and made a point of saying it was the Emperor for whom she acted. They discussed the food situation which, after the lunch he had been given, he must see had become critical. Strutt told her he believed something could be done. All the while they were talking, his brain was rapidly recalibrating the known facts of their situation. His interest had suddenly become engaged since meeting this very unusual

Imperial couple and he had come to a surprising conclusion. Damn it all, but he really was going to have to make the effort to help these people.

Zita noticed that he was wearing the Star of Romania and asked him if he had met Queen Marie? She had heard that the Queen was still a very attractive woman.

Lt Colonel Strutt replied that had had the honour recently – on his way here, as a matter of fact. Looking amused, Zita said she had heard the Queen was very powerful in Romania. Had he met the King as well? Strutt told her yes, but briefly. After he had been introduced to the King, the Queen had invited the King to leave the room. Strutt grinned.

'Not really!?' Zita laughed. 'How awful. How amusing!'

After their chat, the Empress took him down the corridor to meet her mother-in-law, the Archduchess Maria Josefa, the Emperor's mother. Strutt disliked Germans at the best of times and this old woman was simply repulsive – horribly dressed in a shapeless mound of shawls and bedroom slippers. She sat in her over-furnished quarters accompanied by two large mangy dogs who slobbered on his shoes. She might be the sister of the King of Saxony, but she looked what she was – a simple-minded German hausfrau with uncombed hair and few teeth. He struggled not to flinch.

She received him with effusion and gushed all over him. He found it impossible to avoid shaking hands. She insisted on describing the fabulous beauty of her former home called Miramare at Trieste, which she recently was forced to leave. Strutt was so affronted by her, he did not mention he had recently seen Miramare for himself. The Empress, of course, noticed and was secretly amused. He could hardly wait to leave.

Chapter Fifteen

February 28-30, 1919

After his audience with the Empress and back in the now darkened corridor which he now noticed was lined with two oppressive rows of antlers, Strutt had to feel his way along. There were no lights. As he passed the offices, he noticed people working with only one lamp in each room, there was not even a candle on display. When he finally tracked Shonta down, he tripped over a bit of furniture near the office door.

'What is going on here?!' he barked at the Lieutenant 'Who is in charge? Who supplies the castle with food and fuel? Why has the situation been allowed to deteriorate to this state? The Empress has only one light in her room!' Strutt was furious and later wrote it all down in the diary he was keeping for his superiors.

Shonta told him in a confidential voice that it was the Empress who was in charge of everything. She pretended it was the Emperor and they all went along with that. She ordered everything through her two ladies in waiting. They organised the move from Schoenbrunn Palace to Eckartsau three months before. They organised the food and fuel from local suppliers, but these suppliers were now unable or unwilling to sell to them anymore. In two or three weeks they would have nothing.

Curious, Strutt asked what the Empress planned to do then. Shonta was silent for a moment or two, and told him quietly, that before Christmas she had asked her brothers to find help. He heard they had applied to the French President, but had been refused. 'The defeated enemy does not deserve any quarter,' was the reply. Then the brothers went to England to see the King. Shonta watched Strutt as the penny dropped.

And here he was, God help him. Strutt went to the dark window and ruminated on why King George would bother to help an enemy Imperial Family to whom he wasn't related and owed nothing and then he remembered the Romanovs. There had been some faint story about the King countermanding the rescue attempt, but he had paid no attention to it. Now he understood it. The King felt guilty about the Romanovs and so he, Lieutenant Colonel Edward Strutt, must come to the rescue of the Habsburgs. God Almighty! He turned to Shonta. The Empress didn't look entirely well, Shonta told him she was pregnant again. Strutt reeled back. Pregnant and she was pulling this whole load herself!

Suddenly, far off they could hear the sound of gunfire. Shonta told him it was nothing to worry about as poachers roamed the woods most nights. Strutt was furious all over again. Food should not be a problem here. He asked Shonta to make a list immediately of what food and supplies they needed. He waited impatiently for Shonta to comply and then rang up the British Food Commission, which had recently been set up in Vienna. He told them he wanted everything they needed – food and fuel – to be delivered tomorrow and then he handed the telephone over to Shonta who read out the list of requirements.

The next day was wonderfully crisp and clear. After breakfast, Strutt sent up a note to the Empress tactfully suggesting that the Imperial table might like a bit of variety and if so he would be happy to gather a few guns and see if they could do as well as the poachers. The Empress was so struck by this brilliant idea, she came down herself to congratulate him on such a stroke of genius. 'Just what one would expect from His Majesty's representative', she said eyes glowing. Strutt, embarrassed, avoided Ashmore's eye.

Hunyady had taken over the organisation of the guns and while everything was being assembled outside on the drive, the Empress took the opportunity to introduce Strutt to the five Imperial children who were taking the air with their nannies. Otto, the Crown Prince, age six, was a very good-looking boy, dressed in green wool short trousers and a matching little jacket trimmed with red piping and horn buttons. There was intelligence in his eyes. Here was the next Emperor if all goes well, thought Strutt. Otto had his arm around a lovely steel grey wiemaraner who was the Emperor's dog. The Empress introduced him and the dog, Gussel, lifted her paw to shake his hand. He was amused and impressed. Gussel was clearly a superior dog. The little girl, Adelaide, aged nearly five, was wearing a dark blue coat with pretty embroidery on the collar and cuffs. She gave him a shy little smile and a very competent curtsey. Robert, aged three, just looked up at him and grinned. He was a delightful poppet. The other two were still babies. She had a fine family.

The guns were ready; Ledohoffski and a few other gentlemen had joined them. They set off in two parties; one lot in search of deer and the other in search of birds. There was a lot of laughter and camaraderie in the two groups. The Empress chose to go with Strutt. The morning was cloudless, but despite all efforts most of the ducks were flying well out of range. Suddenly, Strutt had a piece of amazing luck. For the first time in his life he managed to bag two woodcock with a left and a right. He was ecstatic and turned to the Empress and cried 'did you see that!' For a moment he looked almost boyish. 'Yes!' she squealed with her hands at her mouth. She was as thrilled as he. With a huge smile, she blurted out 'that was superb. Well done, Colonel! I have never seen it done before.' This was the real Zita, an excited girl.

Strutt laughed and told her he had never done it before. They then exchanged a completely unguarded look, one that only a man and a woman would give when they were attracted to each other. Zita immediately looked down and brightly told him she must run and tell the Emperor. He would be so pleased. She looked up and smiled shyly at him, then went to tell the others.

In the end, they got two roe deer, three mallard, a teal and lost three or four more. Everyone was happy. This had been the best day in a long time and to their surprise the day got even better when they returned to the castle.

In front, on the sweep of the drive, were two big army lorries with British flags fixed to their sides. Everyone went a bit wild, even the Empress. Food at last. Everyone helped unload the boxes. White bread was greeted as a treasure. No one had seen it since 1916. Strutt remarked that it must have been baked in Fiume or even Padua; it wouldn't be fresh, but no one cared. Everyone helped carry the boxes into the castle.

That night there was a special dinner and everyone stood and drank a toast to Colonel Strutt. There was lots of laughter and gaiety and huge relief. The food situation was now dealt with for the present. The tinned bully beef supplied by the British, supplemented by venison and game from the park would see them through. Nobody was going to starve. Zita and the two countesses thanked Strutt once again for coming to their aid.

In the morning, Strutt had another serious discussion with Shonta about their defences and this time he included Count Hunyady, who had once been a soldier. There were only ten Vienna police with them and they were armed with carbines and revolvers, but there was very little ammunition. In addition, there were about twenty armed men who might be of some use if it came to it, plus Ledohoffsky, Ashmore and themselves. Strutt did not believe this would be enough against a determined attack.

Strutt concluded the house was indefensible. It could be silently rushed by twenty armed men in a few minutes. The ground floor windows were barred, but the reception hall with its opposing entrances had only shuttered French windows. The outlook, if there was an attempt on the family, was not reassuring. Shonta told him he had heard between two and three hundred Red Guards with armoured cars were continually cruising around nearby Orth. Hunyady had heard the same, but that turned out to be a gross exaggeration.

The roads were fortunately too wet and heavy for these armoured cars to come into the grounds, but Strutt did subsequently meet one of them on the road himself. It was an unpleasant experience. In this instance, the car did not stop, but he was afraid of what could happen if the Imperial Family were to be accosted by one of them whilst out driving.

He always slept with a revolver under his pillow, but one morning a couple of days later, it occurred to him to test the cartridges. He had had them for some time. So, after breakfast he went out with an eager Ashmore into the grounds, well away from the house and chose a target – a large tree branch. As he rather expected, the gun did not fire. He tried again with the same result. It was a damn good thing he decided to test his cartridges! He told Ashmore to try his. Ashmore had better luck, but not all his cartridges fired either. Studying his pistol, he wanted to know what the cause of this could be. The two men went over to a convenient log and sat down for a think.

Strutt told him he suspected it was the damp conditions over the last few months. The train from Zagreb was practically wringing wet, if he remembered. Ashmore did, he also remembered he was the only dry passenger on that occasion and shot Strutt a teasing look, which was not returned. Strutt was more concerned about where they were going to find replacements for their cartridges.

On the way back to the castle, they ran into Hunyady, who was in a hurry, but stopped to listen and suggested they have a look in the gun room. He'd seen plenty of cartridges there the previous day, but they might not be the right type. He also suggested they should ask the ten policemen what their ammunition supply was and if they might not need a few more cartridges themselves. Strutt was relieved. That was one problem solved. Now where was the gun room?

Back in the entrance hall, he asked a footman to direct them to the gun room. This underling had the effrontery to suggest he first find the gun keeper to assist them. Strutt was not pleased at the delay, but saw the efficacy of this. Shortly, a unshaven old soldier appeared in long leather breeches and high boots. His hair sprang out of his head in thick silver bristles cut short on top, tuffs of hair showed at his ears and around his mouth was a thick black moustache and short beard. He wore the maroon livery of the house.

Bruno Schultz would be delighted to show Strutt and Ashmore the gun room. It was just this way. The two of them followed the older man down the stairs to the lower floor where the estate offices were to be found down a long corridor lined with three rows of antlers above the half-panelling. Bruno told Strutt in a deep gravelly voice how much everyone had enjoyed the shoot the day before. He couldn't think why the Emperor had not suggested doing the same, but the poor man he had been so ill. Strutt made no comment.

They reached the door to the gun room and went in. It was a large room, partially underground with a vaulted ceiling. The windows were about two feet from the ceiling and emitted plenty of light. Again, there was a plethora of antlers lining the upper walls with a particularly fine deer's head over the fireplace. The floor was stone. On each wall there were tall mahogany cupboards and chests filled with hunting paraphernalia. Bruno opened one of the tall cupboards. Inside were several shotguns in superb condition. Strutt asked him how big was the cartridge supply for these guns and for that matter for the guns they had with them. He named a few of them. He only had his pistol as did Ashmore. However, the ten policeman were equipped with both rifles and pistols.

Bruno went over to a chest of drawers, one of several lining the walls, and pulled open the big brass handles. Inside were boxes of ammunition for rifles, shotguns and few for revolvers. He explained the Emperors, had always made sure there was an ample supply of cartridges for his friends in case they hadn't brought enough for their use. There was always someone who needed more.

He went to another cabinet and drew out a superb Borovnik shotgun, made in Ferlach, Carinthia, a southeastern state of Austria. Strutt whistled. They didn't come better that this. The beautifully polished oak stock glowed with a deep rich colour. He had always appreciated finely tooled guns. He ran his fingers over the sidelock handle which resembled a long leaf and the exquisite silver and gold engraving on the side showed two stags running through a field of flowers. He knew full well that the famous Ferlach gunsmiths were to guns what Cartier was to jewellery and he relished it. What a treat.

Next to it, he was surprised to find an English Purdey, another great maker of shotguns and rifles. There were few guns in the world as good as these. He asked Bruno how the English guns compared to those made in Ferlach and was happy to hear that Bruno thought they shot as well, but the engraving was not always up to the same standard. Strutt felt that was fair comment. After looking his fill, he remembered why they had come here and asked Bruno if he could spare enough ammunition to supply their immediate needs. Bruno replied he would ask the Emperor, but he was sure it would be all right. So did Strutt.

Chapter Sixteen

March 2, 1919

As the days went by, several people came out from Vienna to visit. One was the Emperor's doctor, 'a good fellow, but supremely ignorant of the political situation,' according to Strutt's diary. Another was Conradi von Hoetzedorff, late Chief of the Austrian General Staff. He was another larger than life presence with his short grey hair, piercing eyes and thick white moustache. Everyone thought him a brilliant strategist, but Strutt was aware that his major campaigns had all ended in defeat. He greeted Strutt very cordially and spoke much of British gallantry in Italy.

'Without doubt, you and the French, but especially your men, saved the situation for those miserable Italian cowards,' was one of the General's first remarks. Strutt had already noted the extreme prejudice that most Allied military men felt against the Italian army. Indeed, it seemed to be the universal opinion throughout Austria-Hungary, French, Serbian and Greek circles. He knew it wasn't true in all cases. Many Italian regiments had acquitted themselves well, but obviously enough didn't and that left an impression.

After five days had elapsed since his arrival, Strutt went to Vienna in search of messages. He drove out in the huge open Daimler, accompanied by Countess Bellegarde and Ledo. Both of them were wearing goggles as they were in the back seat. The Countess had also swathed her head and face with a gauze veil. Ledo had on his greatcoat with the deep fur collar and hat. Before they left, Strutt thanked the driver for painting out the imperial crests on the doors. It was a small thing, but a prudent one.

The drive was uneventful; having to shout to communicate in the open air at one's companions did not lend itself to much conversation. Once in Vienna, Strutt dropped them off at Schoenbrunn Palace and continued on to the British Embassy. There he found that Cuninghame and his cipher clerk were still in Prague, but the secretary was there to show him several telegrams. Unfortunately, they were in cipher and he would have to wait until Cuninghame returned. Strutt felt angry and frustrated.

As his business was over earlier than expected, he decided to visit some old friends, Prince and Princess Festetics, whose house was not far away. They had always been great friends and seeing them would cheer him up. He duly drove round to their house and rang the doorbell. After a minute or so, the ornate front door was opened to display two rows of bowing, powdered footmen in silk livery with knee breeches. Strutt was so surprised by the sight, he barked out a laugh.

It was then that his friend, Prince Taszilo Festetics, came into the hall and seeing him, shouted 'Bill, how delightful to see you, my friend! Come in. Come in.' Strutt queried the footmen with his hands and Festetics told him that the display was his way of defying the times. They were also very useful for finding food!

In the ornate drawing room, Strutt found Taszilo's younger brother George lounging about with a couple of friends drinking coffee. They all warmly welcomed him. George was a diplomat, but had fought in the Austro-Italian campaign. He looked gaunt and tired. Strutt noticed the magnificent ceiling. He had forgotten about it. The whole of it was entirely lined with gilt framed oil paintings which gave the room a deeper richness than normal. Of course, the rest of the room was beautifully furnished with the usual French marquetry tables, carved mirrors and what not. Strutt deeply appreciated that the whole looked very well cared for and undamaged.

The friends were discussing the Bolshevik problem again. It was like a cancer, George said unhappily, like a disease. The first people it seemed to affect were small bureaucrats. Taszilo agreed, but it wasn't just bureaucrats. When the Russians released the Austro-Hungarian prisoners of war, they knew what they were doing. Most of them, who hated the Emperor anyway for not stopping the war, were now also firm Communists and there were more than a million of them coming their way!

One of the friends told him a story about Princess Lonyay's daughter's house being invaded by Red Guards. Strutt frowned. This lady was one of the highest in the land. Born Princess Stephanie of Belgium, she was the widow of Crown Prince Archduke Rudolph von Habsburg, by whom she had a daughter married to Prince Otto zu Windisch-Gratz. Later she married Prince Lonyay, the German ambassador to Vienna. It seemed Bolsheviks in the countryside were becoming an increasing problem. Not to be ignored.

Taszilo manoeuvred him into a corner to whisper that he was worried about the Emperor being at Eckartsau unprotected. Strutt told him there were no worries as yet on that score. He then asked them all if the current crew of republicans in power could be got rid of, would the people welcome the Emperor back? He thought he would test the water. Taszilo, George and the friends thought not. It was too late. The people blamed him for making things worse and for being weak. The world had changed, they all nodded in agreement.

George tried to explain. It was Franz Joseph who kept the Empire together by treating all the different nationalities in the Empire equally, even the Jews. It was quite a feat, but the old man was blind when it came to nationalism. Since he died, this had unravelled. The new young Emperor had a lot of the right ideas, but not the force of character to carry them through and anyway the times were wrong for him. The war had smashed the Empire. The creaking, feudal structure had collapsed. Somehow they were all going to have to start again...without the Emperor. Strutt felt his own opinion confirmed, having met Karl. He was the wrong man for the times. It would take a Napoleon to turn things around here.

On the way back to his car around mid-day, a trim, well-dressed lady fainted on the pavement in front of him. Strutt stopped and looked about. She seemed to be unaccompanied. He knelt down to see what he could do. Her face was chalk white, but otherwise, she seemed all right and indeed after a few moments, her eyes opened. He raised her to lean against his knee and asked her when she had last had a meal?

Weakly, she told him not for a day or two. She tried to get up. Strutt grimaced. He'd seen this before, too many times. Telling her she could trust him, he picked her up and carried her to his car. His startled driver, leapt out and opened the door so he could put her into the back seat. Strutt directed him to drive them to the British Food Commission immediately. It turned out to be a large warehouse at the north of town. He hadn't yet been there, but the driver knew the way.

Inside the warehouse, they found huge boxes of food parcels sent out from Britain to feed British prisoners in Turkey and Bulgaria, but as these were no longer needed owing to the Armistice, the Red Cross was seeing to their distribution locally. Strutt escorted the very grateful woman to a table where there was a chair and asked one of the commissioners to feed her immediately and give her some supplies. It went across the grain for him to just leave her there, so after a pause to consider, he went to find an officer and arranged for her to be driven home later. He could do no more. Courteously he said goodbye to her and quickly made an exit before she could flood him with more tears and thanks. It was time for something cheerful.

Chapter Seventeen

March 2, 1919
The Tyre Incident

He rejoined his car and directed the driver to take him round to see Countess Yella Szecheny, an old friend who was the world's greatest intriguer and gossip. He remembered her as an attractive, tiny figure probably in her late thirties who was invariably present wherever interesting people gathered. She could drink most men under the table and dance all night while she was at it. Yella was great fun.

When he arrived at her large apartment overlooking one of the most elegant squares in the city, he thought she had rather lost her looks since he had seen her two years before, but her bright green eyes and rasping whisky voice were the same. She greeted him with thrills of delight in her silver-grey salon and implored him to stay for a bite to eat. Her perpetual cigarette in its holder made arcs of smoke in the air as she gestured.

Yella had a mischievous triangular face under frizzy hennaed hair, her eyelashes were darkened with mascara, her lips were slashed with red and at her ears she wore a slim pair of swinging emerald coloured stones. To complete the look, she wore a bright green Chinese style silk kimono belted at the waist with a gold sash. She talked all the time, making him laugh with her continual malapropisms in both German and French. She couldn't seem to help it. This day she was very depressed about the political situation and worried about her 'dear Archduke Eugen', the Emperor's brother. She was also full of questions and scandals, with Strutt laughed and paid strict attention.

Yella had always loved fur and so there was a tiger skin on the floor in front of the fire and a few threadbare creatures thrown over antique sofas and chairs. He craned his neck to see if the Tree was still there in the sunny side room. It was. The tree, an orange tree, had been given to Yella years before in a large pot by a nephew. It was then about a meter in height. Over the years, Yella had loved it like a child and nurtured it until now it had grown to fill most of the room, floor to ceiling and wall to wall. It even had a name: Hugo. Strutt didn't know what had happened to her husband, Count Heinrich von Haugwitz. She seemed to have mislaid him. There were no children as far as he knew.

Over tiny cups of coffee and a sandwich brought to them by a shabbily dressed maid with a wrinkled apron, she regaled him with a marvellous supply of gossip, most of which was possibly true. This was useful information. Over the course of a few visits, Strutt was able to frame with surprising accuracy how the current Provisional Government of Renner, Bauer and company actually worked. These men were now the rulers of the country and Strutt knew it would be wise to find out as much about them as he could, just in case. Yella told him Karl Renner came originally from a tiny village in Moravia, where his family owned a poor vineyard. She didn't know how many children there were. Anyway, Renner turned out to be intelligent, so much so that he was picked out to attend a gymnasium (a sort of higher school) where he did very well. After that he studied Law somewhere. Later he became a socialist and got into politics. He was clever. Now he was leader of the Social Democratic Party and if what they say is true, he will shortly be leader of the new Republic.

This was the first time Strutt had heard a Republic mentioned. Who was behind it, did she know? Yella replied that all the socialist parties wanted it. The Empire was dead. They wanted power now. Strutt asked her what Renner thought of the Emperor? Would he allow him to stay in Austria if he abdicated? Yella wasn't sure, maybe he would be allowed to stay as a private citizen, but what about his wealth? She didn't know.

Strutt pressed her to describe Otto Bauer, who was currently Minister of Foreign Affairs. Yella made a face. He was a nasty man. Bauer was on the left of the Social Democratic Party, having spent time as a prisoner of war in Russia. It was Bauer who had just signed the Anschluss agreement joining Austria to Germany.[1] Yella shook her head when she said this. The Allies will not let it stand, she said, as it would make Germany too powerful.

After bidding the Countess farewell for the present and admiring Hugo who had sprouted a few early buds in his warm room, he drove on

---

1. This was a secret agreement signed 2 March, 1919. It didn't last.

to collect Countess Bellegarde and Count Ledohoffski at Schoenbrunn Palace. They had had a decent lunch and a nice visit with friends. As before, they sat in the back of the open Daimler with Strutt in front with the driver. The road home in mid-afternoon, followed beside a railway track for a few miles. The Countess' clothes and hat were quite distinctive and the painted-out crests on the doors were perhaps a little too obvious.

Shortly a train caught up with them with a lot of noise and flying smoke. It was full of rowdy demobilised Austrian soldiers who thought they recognised the Imperial Couple in the back seat of the car. Both Ledo and the Countess tried their best to be unconcerned and inconspicuous, but this didn't stop the soldiers from shouting out insults which became more and more aggressive as the train passed them. Strutt saw an officer put his hand on his pistol. At this dangerous point, their car suddenly jerked sideways with a tyre puncture and they were forced to slow down and stop – just as the train came to a halt fifteen yards away at a small siding to let people out. There was a small station, but no village was in sight. Strutt's driver apologised abjectly. 'It's the tyres, Excellenz. Since the war, they are not good.'

Strutt got out of the car and faced the jeering Austrians. He put a keen eye on the officer with the pistol. Strutt then let rip with an electrifying tirade in German which silenced all of them. The officer put his hand down, but still looked menacing. Strutt carefully noted that he wore a dust-covered uniform with unpolished boots and looked like he might be in his late twenties. There was brown hair with a widow's peak and dark eyes in a square face, and in those eyes Strutt saw no respect at all. If he wasn't a Bolshevik already, Strutt figured he soon would be. A few of the soldiers bowed their heads and said '*Un verzeihung, Excellenz* (pardon us).'

Strutt barked out a demand for 'volunteers' to change the punctured tyre. Three men climbed down and changed the tyre, while the menacing officer turned his back, but not before Strutt had seen the sneer on his face. It was all done in minutes. The train then left with some of the young soldiers saluting them from a window. The officer made a rude gesture at Strutt as the Daimler proceeded on its way. Only then did Countess Bellegarde break into semi-hysterical laughter which she had been suppressing at Strutt's unbelievable audacity. Ledo was white around the gills and near to fainting. Both knew the interlude might have ended differently.

Chapter Eighteen

March 3, 1919
A Buggy Ride

The next afternoon, the Emperor invited Strutt for a drive in his smart black gig with yellow wheels pulled by a handsome black mare. It was a lovely winter's day, cold with bright sunshine. They drove over damp tracks for two hours and Strutt listened while the Emperor talked.

Karl told him when he came to the throne, he had wanted to be a modern, democratic monarch. That was his ideal. The byzantine structure his great uncle had run was way out of date and needed to brought up to the twentieth century. He wanted to be a constitutional monarch within a federal frame work. He did find some support, but it became clear it just wasn't possible to transform the Empire in the middle of a war. Or at any time, was Strutt's thought.

They spoke of '*boche*' atrocities and the sinking of hospital ships. Despite everything, the Emperor still believed his former German allies had some honour left. He would not believe that they would attack hospital ships. Strutt might tell him that they pillaged, murdered and did every other outrage. That he could believe because they did it in his country, too, but surely they would not dare sink hospital ships?

Strutt eventually convinced him it was true, because the British Salonika hospital ships were the principal victims of the German U boats towards the end. He knew it from personal experience. The Emperor hung his head in regret, he was so sorry.

They spoke of Sarajevo and the Emperor perked up and told him he did not believe the Serbs were really guilty of starting the war. Strutt stared into the distance. Was it fair, queried the Emperor, to blame a whole nation just because one crazed Serb assassinated Archduke Ferdinand and his wife?

Strutt tried to edge off this dangerous subject. The Emperor had a reasonable, if irrelevant point, but he did not want to get into any discussion

Die Kinder von Kaiser Karl und Kaiserin Zita.

Karl and Zita's children. (From left to right) Elizabeth, Charlotte, Rudolf, Karl Ludwig, Felix, Robert, Adelheid, Otto.

Count Jozsef Hunyady.

Count Ottokar Czernin. (© *Library of Congress*)

Countess Gabriella von Bellegarde.

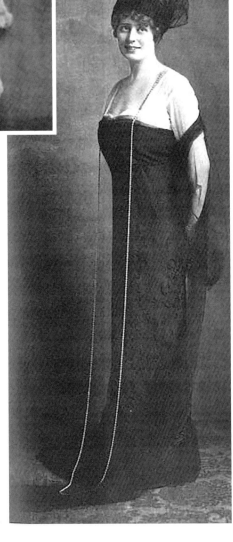

Countess Agnes Schoenborn, c. 1912.

Eckartsau Castle.

Emperor Karl I of Austria-Hungary.

General Henri Mathias Berthelot.

Queen Marie of Romania.

Schloss Wartegg, Switz.

The wedding of Zita and Karl,
21 October 1911.

Empress Zita of Austria-Hungary. (© *Harris & Ewing Collection*)

about Austria's culpability for starting the war. Instead, he changed the subject by asking Karl what had happened to Franz Ferdinand's children. There were three of them, he recalled.

The Emperor was happy to diverge from the subject of war for the moment. The children were all right, thank goodness. Of course, the whole thing had been a horrible shock. Franz' sister-in-law was looking after them at their home at Konopie near Prague. They were still young. The girl wasn't married yet and the two boys were still at school.

Strutt remembered her, Baroness Henriette Chotek, was that her name? He seemed to recall a sweet-faced woman. The Archduke had introduced them once at San Moritz. He didn't think she enjoyed the skiing much, as he never saw her there again.

The Emperor would not be put off discussing the war, however, and carried on. Strutt was uneasy about this and wished he would stop. Being made party to a recitation of past stupidities was depressing and not a little embarrassing. He steeled himself. The Emperor clearly wanted to unburden himself.

He told him how when he came to the throne, his only thought was to stop the war. It was killing the people. He hated it. After the Brusilov Offensive in the summer of 1916, his army had taken such a beating, he didn't think it would ever recover. He had to make the war stop.

Strutt remembered the battle well. He wasn't involved, but he knew many who were. This battle took place in present-day Ukraine in the general vicinity of Lviv, Kovel and Lutsk. It was the biggest Russian offensive on the Eastern Front and it was hugely successful. Sadly, it was the Emperor's army which had taken the majority of the nearly 800,000 casualties.

Karl became visibly distressed. Nearly a million men died. It hurt him to think of it, yet he couldn't seem to stop. He fished in his pocket for his handkerchief and wiped his eyes. He then went on to relate how he had tried to stop the war by directly negotiating with the French. He had thought if he could get the French to agree, then together, they would have a better chance of persuading the Germans to agree as well. Zita thought it was a good idea and so did her brother Prince Sixtus. Unfortunately, it all went disastrously wrong.

Strutt could do nothing but stare ahead and wonder at the conceit of kings. Did the Emperor not realise that after his armies were smashed to pieces by General Brusilov, that he had no power left to do anything? How is it he did not accept that he was utterly defeated? Perhaps he felt that as Germany was his ally, all was not yet lost. But then how dare he go behind Germany's back to sue for peace?

After an hour of driving along snow-covered paths, Karl turned the gig around and headed back a slightly different way. Under the clear skies, the Danube was looking very blue. The remains of the ice blocks had almost melted. Strutt noticed no signs of spring yet, but there was a silence as if the empty branches were gathering strength to put out shoots.

He was angry and embarrassed about being forced to listen to Karl's confessions. He felt an urge to remonstrate, to shout even, but he contained himself. He knew full well there was nothing the young Emperor could have done to bring a halt to the war. If he had made things temporarily worse, well it was only himself and Austria that suffered.

The Emperor smiled boyishly at him. He didn't know why he was telling Strutt all this. Perhaps he thought an outside opinion might present a different point of view. Strutt was instantly alarmed, but before he could think of a comment, the Emperor continued.

One thing was for sure. He had been incredibly lucky to have secured the Empress as his wife. Believe it or not, he told Strutt, she was of enormous help to him. She may not look it, because she was so modest and sweet, but she was very quick to understand even quite complicated issues. Then he asked Strutt if he was married? Strutt reeled for a moment, taken aback by the Emperor's lack of understanding of his own wife, then admitted he was.

The Emperor was pleased to hear it. 'Then you know how difficult it can be not to disappoint the people who love you?' Strutt winced internally. This discussion was getting far too personal. He nodded in sympathy realizing this well-meaning, weak man was giving him a huge compliment by telling him all this.

'In the end,' went on Karl, 'due to treachery, all we managed to do was make matters far worse than they were. The Germans in effect took over my country and the remains of my army! I couldn't stop them. Now we really don't know what is going to happen, but I do think we are safe here for the present.'

Strutt decided to ignore all references to the Sixtus Affair. They would be in deep water there. However, for his own safety, he felt it necessary that the Emperor must understand a few facts. Bracing himself, Strutt told Karl he was correct in believing they were safe here when they first came some months ago, but he was not at all convinced this was still the case. He was told on all sides that the Bolsheviks were more numerous and getting nearer every day and he had been told that while the Emperor was loved by many of the people, the current Republican government was hostile to him. He should, in short, give serious thought to leaving the country soon.

The Emperor did not take this well and replied quite sharply. There was certainly no need to think of that yet and what ever happened, he would never abdicate. Again and again, he reiterated to Strutt that he had not abdicated. 'I went into retirement on 3 November, 1918 pending the restoration of order. I am still Emperor.' Strutt wrote this down in his diary later.

After some reflection, he asked Strutt what he thought of the idea of him writing to King George and Lloyd George, asking them to dispatch British troops to Austria-Hungary? All they needed were two divisions for Budapest to control Hungary and one for Linz and Vienna. Ten thousand men, even five thousand would do. His knew his officers were still loyal and they would organise what was left of his old armies behind Strutt's. If they couldn't send British troops, they could send Americans.

At this point, they found themselves having to deal with a low-hanging branch. Strutt stood up in his seat to lift it over them. He felt a headache starting, but there was to be no respite. The Emperor had not yet come to the end of his confessions. He wanted Strutt to understand how he had truly tried to do the right things. First, he had attempted to rule autocratically and when that didn't work, he gave democracy a go. It turned out both were big mistakes, but of the two the latter was by far the greatest.

Strutt asked how that came about, knowing he was going to be told anyway.

The Emperor wanted to prove to everyone that he was deadly earnest about making the country more democratic, so he ordered an amnesty of all political prisoners. He thought in doing so they would see he was on their side but alas it didn't work out that way. He was unable to convince the government to push through the programme of political change that was needed to recast the Empire into a more democratic mould. Without that, the people all thought he had betrayed them. They were more furious than ever.

Lord, thought Strutt, the foolish man had tried to push through an enormously ambitious programme in the midst of the worst war ever. Even in peace time, it would have been a challenge. He commiserated with him at the same time wondered at such incompetence and delusion. Karl was a good man. Strutt was convinced of it. He had been desperate to do the best for his country, indeed he had been prepared to take great risks to do so, but his understanding of the basic facts was sadly wanting. Normally, Strutt would despise such a weak man, but he couldn't as the Emperor radiated such warmth, goodness and charm, he couldn't help liking him. Or maybe he just felt sorry for him. He had to admit, however, that whatever transpired, Karl had done his best. It was a depressing thought.

The fine black horse pulling the Emperor's little gig drew to a stop where the lane gave out at a small inlet. Here they came upon some fishermen hauling up the catch in a seine net and stopped to watch them. The wind had come up a bit to toss the foam on the waves.

The men took off their caps politely. The Emperor, who was dressed in a Field Marshal's dress uniform, urged them in a very friendly fashion to carry on. The resulting catch was sadly not much, just three coarse fish. The Emperor, nevertheless, made much of their effort and thereupon resolved to buy the fish. Unfortunately, patting his pockets, he realised he had no money with him, so he borrowed 20 krona from Strutt, which was more than the fish were worth. Strutt smilingly agreed it was a worthy cause and graciously handed over the money. After conversing for a few minutes, they drove off with the happy gratitude of the men ringing in their ears. They had been delighted to meet their Emperor.

Shortly after starting back, Strutt was immensely relieved to see the Empress, Ledo and Countess Bellegarde strolling through the woods. The Emperor hailed them gaily and pulled up. He suggested that Ledo climb up and take over the reins for him, as he wanted to walk. Strutt got down and let the Empress persuade her husband it was too far for him to walk back to the Castle. Strutt therefore had the pleasure of escorting the two ladies back himself. He had learned much from the gentle Emperor, but keeping his temper and face straight had been an ordeal.

That night, after dinner Strutt wrote of the day's events and more into a report he sent by the Prague diplomatic bag – his only means of communication with home. He addressed his letters to Leo Amery[1] and Lord Bradford at the Foreign Office.[2] To Bradford, he also enclosed Albert Mensdorff's private notes for King George. Count Albert Mensdorff-Pouilly-Dietrichsteinff was a deeply experienced diplomat who wanted to inform the King personally about several matters which he and Strutt both considered very important. It later turned out that the letter, but not the enclosures reached Bradford. Subsequently, the enclosures were found in Curzon of Kedleston's pocket, Strutt rather doubted the King ever saw either. He became convinced that his letters were opened by the censor, in spite of their destination and contents. This was not good.

The Censor later apologised to Lord Bradford, but stated in excuse that Colonel Strutt had once written a most indiscreet letter to Lady Evelyn Cotterell,[3] hence their surveillance. This was rubbish, he would never have divulged anything vital in what was merely a chatty letter. Furthermore, he always sent his private letters by King's Messenger and not the diplomatic bag which meant this route was also being censored.

Far worse than being censored, however, was discovering the Foreign Office was not acknowledging receipt of his telegrams. This was a blow. He had naturally expected the Foreign Office would read and reply to his messages. Now he realised what he had suspected some days ago – on this mission, he really was on his own. Years later, he asked Lord Balfour why his messages were not answered. Balfour replied 'My dear man, how could we acknowledge receipt of them when we could not acknowledge you?'

---

1. Leo Amery 1873-1955. Influential British Conservative MP and journalist.
2. Lt Colonel Orlando Bridgeman, 5th Earl of Bradford 1873-1957. Conservative politician and soldier. Assistant Private Secretary to Robert Gascoyne-Cecil, 3rd Marquis of Salisbury. Later Private Secretary to Prime Minister Arthur Balfour. In 1919 he was the government's Chief Whip in the House of Lords.
3. Lady Evelyn Cotterell. 1872-1922. Daughter of 7th Duke of Richmond. A family friend.

Chapter Nineteen

March 4, 1919

The next week went by slowly. Living at Eckartsau, Strutt decided, was like living in a rather crowded hotel. Walking to and from his room, he could sometimes see through cracks in open doors that other bedrooms were stuffed with beds and luggage sometimes overflowed into the corridor. He strongly suspected more than one person, perhaps many, had been turned out to give him sole occupancy of his magnificent room. He knew Ashmore was sharing with someone.

The castle had been built to house large shooting parties. In the ordinary course, this would require say sixteen bedrooms with additional servants' beds in the attic. From the number of people in the dining room at night, there were clearly some sixty people in residence and most of them would have brought at least one servant. There were one or two small outbuildings in the grounds he had noticed. Maybe some of them were kennelled up there.

As far as he could ascertain, the court consisted mainly of functionaries from Schoenbrunn, distant relatives both old and young, some soldier friends of the Emperor and hangers-on who had lived at the Palace for years. They were 'family' in the way a regiment accrued camp followers if it stayed too long in one place.

He rose at 7.30 after Ashmore woke him with a cup of tea and pulled the curtains. By 8.30 he had made his way downstairs for breakfast in the main dining room. One helped oneself from a large buffet and sat wherever, it was a very informal meal. People came and went. Afterwards, he would make his way to Shonta's office to see what the schedule for the day was.

Lt von Seedak was a very resourceful fellow. He spoke decent English when required, but naturally preferred German. He was the Emperor's acting Intelligence and Communications Officer. Every message to and from the outside world, went through his hands. One day he asked Shonta just how a naval officer had wound up here.

Shonta put down the telephone and smiled. It was a long story, which he would make short. Strutt may recall the last great naval battle in the Adriatic in June 1918 when the Imperial Austrian Navy had tried to blast its way through the Otranto Barrage at the Strait of Otranto. The Allies had put everything into this effort: four dreadnoughts, four destroyers, four torpedo boats, U-boats and even airplanes. Unfortunately, it was not enough to get through the combined French and British fleets. When the *Szentistvan* sank, Shonta had been pulled badly hurt from the water by the crew of what had been the Emperor's yacht and he was taken to Schoenbrunn to recuperate. When the Imperial Couple decided to decamp to Eckartsau, there was need of a Communications Officer and so here he was.

Strutt was impressed. He had forgotten that before the war, the Imperial Austrian navy was one of the largest in the Adriatic and indeed in the whole Mediterranean. They had numerous excellent ports at Trieste, Pola, Fiume and Ragusa, now all lost. Well, he thought, the mighty have fallen everywhere.

He spent a pleasant afternoon driving around the lanes with Count Hunyady who was preoccupied with the intolerable delay of his marriage to Gabriella Bellegarde. Strutt was amused by this. Hunyady didn't strike him as a man passionately in love. He seemed far too reserved. They had planned to marry this coming May at her home near Vienna, but with everything up in the air, they feared it would be postponed. He was also worried about the political situation in Hungary and they discussed it at length. The current government wasn't interested in Austria-Hungary – only in Austria and most of the socialists wanted to unite with German to make one state. In fact the two countries had just signed an Anschluss agreement to that effect,[1] but whether this would be allowed to stand in the Treaty to come, was a moot point.

Strutt found this very interesting. He had heard rumours about it, of course, but he had not heard an Agreement had been signed. He wondered how this would affect the Emperor's position? It certainly did not bode well.

Hunyady pressed Strutt for details about his career. Had he joined the army straight out of school? Strutt admitted he had pretty much.

---

1. Signed on March 2, 1919.

It was that or business or the church. He could have joined the family business, but his father had been a soldier, so he too joined the Royal Scots Fusiliers when he was eighteen. He hadn't regretted it. When he wasn't engaged on army business, he climbed mountains. Hunyady was delighted to hear this and wanted to know more. In the end, they had an interesting afternoon and came back friends.

Another afternoon, he had a walk with Countess Bellegarde. She caught him unawares as he was tramping along the river and challenged him with laughing eyes to a rather long hike which he loved. She was a delightful companion with her fresh open looks and fine dark eyes. At last, after a walking a spell at a furious pace he cried halt and they stopped for a cigarette.

She also was anxious about her marriage. She and Joseph Hunyady had become engaged just before Christmas when they were staying at Schoenbrunn Palace with the Imperial Family. Their engagement had brought a bloom of happiness to everyone at such a dark time. Yes, there was a bit of a gap in their ages – she was only twenty-seven, but neither cared. Hunyady was in his early forties, but he looked considerably younger. A dashing golden brown moustache adorned his upper lip. In repose his face could look severe, but when he smiled his brown eyes sparkled and one realised he looked not only a very capable fellow, but a kind one as well. Strutt liked him.

Part of the draw between them he surmised, watching her animation, was their devotion to the Imperial Couple. Hunyady had been with the Emperor since his first days in the cavalry. He not only respected him, but he loved him. Gabriella felt the same way towards the Empress, whom she had known since they were children playing together at Schwarzau Castle in Lower Austria. Strutt felt pretty confident they would be happy together. Florrie was the one who usually worked these things out, but it seemed reasonable.

Twice during the week, Strutt was invited to a nursery tea by the Empress. These seemed to be bi-weekly occurrences organised by Countess Agnes Schoenborn, who was not only a lady in waiting, but also the Empress' cousin. All the small children in the castle and their mothers were included. Strutt hardly knew what to do with himself. Mercifully, the Emperor with Gussel in tow joined him after a few interminable minutes. After they all had tea and cakes of several sorts, there were games for the children and the screaming began. Gussel, feeling Strutt's discomfort, came over and put his head on his knee and rolled out waves of sympathy from his lustrous brown eyes directly into his. Strutt put his hand on Gussel's sleek head and smiled in appreciation.

On the second occasion that Strutt was invited, he was taken aback when the three older Habsburg children came up to show him a rather clever wooden puzzle box. They wanted to open it. Strutt immediately looked at the Empress for help and she told him he had to find the secret slide which was the first of many such which opened the box. Otto shouted to his mother not to give it all away! Thus challenged, Strutt sat up straight and gruffly prepared to do battle. Robert clutched his knee. Having ascertained in a few minutes what must be the secret, he then made an enormous production of looking for the correct way in. There were many false starts and mistakes. The children got more and more excited, urging him on. Finally he found the way and they were all hugely pleased. The Empress laughed with them, her eyes shining.

On Thursday, they heard the faint sounds of heavy firing again from the direction of Pressburg, this time it sounded like machine guns as well as rifles. Herr Schager, the resident States Councillor, told him not to worry as it was probably local fighting between the free Czechs and the Hungarian Bolsheviks. They were fighting for control of the city. Strutt was unsettled. Trouble was getting closer.

On Friday, Strutt attended a conference in the Emperor's office with the Emperor, Herr Schager and Count Hunyady. This time they spoke about state affairs which Herr Schager reported was bad and deteriorating. To the Emperor's consternation, he announced there were signs that the Provisional Government might soon make Austria a republic. The Emperor couldn't believe it and he and Count Hunyady had a difficult time convincing him it was true. Strutt felt a dread that time was running out and he still had no idea what could be done. Schager further told them he had heard that Bolshevism was increasing in Hungary, but this information was coming from a Bulgarian source, so Strutt couldn't be sure of its veracity.

At this point, the Empress joined them and the conversation turned away from serious matters to King Ferdinand of Bulgaria, who was considered a friend both by the Emperor and Empress. They were both so glad when his son, Boris, took the throne after his father's abdication in December. The conversation turned again to reminiscences, which it often did.

She reminded the Emperor about the state visit they had made to Constantinople in May 1918 to further cement relations with their ally the Turks. They had taken the two Countesses and a large following. Zita had loved it, because it was the first time ladies had been included in an official capacity. In fact, she had dazzled the city with her wonderful jewels, fashionable clothes, and sweet smiles.

She asked Strutt whether his British Salonika Force had been aware of their visit as they expected to be bombed at any minute. Strutt assured her that, of course, their intelligence had known they were there and that strict orders had been issued by General Milne to suspend all air raids during their visit. Strutt had no idea if this was true, but doubted it.

The Emperor asked him to describe what sort of man was General Milne and Strutt told them all about 'Uncle George' as he was affectionately known. He commanded the universal respect of all who knew him. The Herr Schager then said they had heard Milne had been in line for the job of Supreme Commander in the Balkans, but instead the post had gone to General d'Esperey. Why was that?

Strutt was surprised to find his erstwhile enemies so well informed about two men he knew well. He told them either general would have done the job effectively, but the British Salonika Force faced such particularly difficult problems, it was decided the more experienced commander was needed there.

They immediately wanted to know what those problems were. Strutt laughed. Heavens, where to start? In the first place, Macedonia was completely unprepared for war and by that he meant there was no proper infrastructure. There were no decent roads, few trains and those inadequate, little food, no water supplies, no maps even. Everything had to be brought in by sea. Thousands and thousands of horses and mules had to be found, along with their fodder. On top of all that, there was rampant malaria.

The Empress put her hand to her throat, her eyes widened. She had had no idea. Seeing this, Strutt lightened the tone by entertaining them with the story of how they managed to find a Greek peasant who was a water diviner. Did they know what that is? Strutt explained. A water diviner is someone who, by instinct, knows where to dig for water. Their man did it by walking around holding a thin elbow-shaped branch in front of him. Strutt demonstrated with two pencils. The branch would drop down automatically when it found water under the ground. The Emperor was amused, but didn't believe it. Strutt assured him that it was true. Nine times out of ten they found water and when they didn't it was because the water was just too far down to make it worthwhile digging any further.

The Empress was amazed and asked him how many wells they had to dig. The whole room was silenced when he told them the number all told was probably well over a hundred. After that, he tried to edge off the subject, but it became clear that the Emperor did not want to discuss the deteriorating national situation in front of the Empress. The Emperor urged him to tell them more, so finally Strutt bored them with tales of laying tracks through the mountains and that ended the meeting.

The days passed and Strutt spent his time talking to the men and writing letters, which he worried would not get through. It had taken a little time before he fully accepted they were being censored and would not be acknowledged. He still visited the Embassy regularly hoping for messages. One glorious day there was a package waiting there for him. It contained small clothes, shirts, two pairs of plus-fours, pajamas and four pairs of socks from Florrie. He was thrilled. That woman had a genius for getting supplies to him when he most needed them.

He often stopped for tea and gossip with Yella Szechenyi and did not neglect his other friends. As Kary Czernin was in disgrace with the Emperor, he tactfully made sure that his car never stood outside his house in daylight.

On March 11, there was a humorous story in the newspapers. The Italian Mission had declared its intention of commandeering two paintings at Eckartsau of d'Este[2] origin, the property of the Emperor. These pictures possessed little merit beyond family interest, but as Strutt knew the Italians were busy looting the Vienna museums of any works of art of Italian origin, these pictures were presumably on their list. The papers all stated that the Italians had proceeded to Eckartsau to get the paintings and had been very badly received by Lt Colonel Strutt who

---

2. The Este family were the ruling family of the city of Ferrarra in Italy during the 15th and 16th centuries.

showed them the door in the 'harshest' fashion!' Everyone at Eckartsau was amused, except Strutt who hadn't realised his presence at the hunting lodge was so well known. Needless to say, the Italians never came and they denied the story officially two days later. Strutt took it as a warning.

On March 12, the Emperor was visited by his brother Archduke Maximillian Eugen and his wife Archduchess Franziska (nee Hohenlohe). Both of them were very young and exceedingly good looking. Strutt had known Franzy as a child and was pleased to see her again all grown up. They greeted him very cordially.

The next day, Mr Butler, the British Food Commissioner for Austria-Hungry and the new Yugoslav states dropped by to see if they had sufficient for their needs. He was, of course, greeted with enormous gratitude and effusion of thanks by Count Hunyady who invited him to stay for dinner at the request of the Emperor. Butler, whom Strutt described as a 'fat, well-fed man of the London City merchant type,' was gratified to accept the invitation despite it meaning a two hour return journey in the dark.

This immediately threw the Court into an excited flurry. Who should have the honour of sitting on the Empress' right, Colonel Strutt or Mr Butler? They wished to honour him for the continuing largesse of the Food Commission, but on the other hand the Colonel had garnered enormous gratitude and respect since he had come amongst them. They didn't want to slight him. Eventually, it was decided that Strutt should have the greater honour and Mr Butler was consigned to her left.

After a very good dinner of roast venison and a divine apfulstrudel topped with vanilla ice cream, Strutt gleaned from Butler, whom he had not met previously, that the British Food Commission was providing Vienna with five to ten tonnes of food per week. It was all they could manage and very generous. This was excellent news. Butler then told him that their opposite number, the American Mission, with hundreds of officers all over the country and at least thirty men in Vienna alone, had promised only a thousand tonnes a week and so far even these had not turned up.

This was astounding news, considering their huge resources. Strutt was further surprised much later to learn that up to the time of his leaving Austria, while the British tonnes were regularly sent, the Americans had still not delivered anything. Strutt noted in his diary with extreme prejudice: 'The Food Commission was like their Red Cross, just propaganda and in Austria damned bad propaganda, too.' Obviously, American aid did not stretch as far as Austria in the early days of 1919.

The next day found him back in Vienna. Disappointingly, there was still no means of deciphering the telegrams that had come in. As he was talking to one of the secretaries, a messenger came in and gave him a note from Princess Lonyay asking him to come and see her. He duly went around to her house and was effusively greeted and invited to stay for lunch. She looked very well, not altered at all since he had last seen her in 1914, but she talked more than ever. She was an attractive brunette and looked very well, not altered at all since he had last seen her in 1914. Born Princess Stephanie of Belgium, she had married Crown Prince Rudolph of Austria-Hungary at seventeen. It was a brilliant match, but unfortunately not a success as Rudolph was mentally unstable. They had a daughter together in 1883, but no more children. In 1889, he committed suicide at the hunting lodge at Mayerling after murdering his young mistress, Baroness Mary Vetsera. It was a huge tragedy which was thoroughly hushed up. Very few people knew what had actually happened. Much bruised by this nasty affair, Stephanie did not marry again until 1900. This time she chose for herself and got it right. Her new husband, Prince Elmer Lonyay, had made her happy.

At lunch this day, she was on her own with Prince Lonyay's young nephew who had been very badly wounded in battle just a few weeks before the end of the war. He was still in a bad way, but nevertheless eager to get back into action. Half lying on a cushioned chaise by the window, the young man quizzed Strutt on the possibility of his enlisting in the British Foreign Legion. Strutt just smiled. He told the Empress later that he had the devil of a time convincing the young cub that there was no such thing as the British Foreign Legion. The boy was bitterly disappointed.

Soon another guest joined them – Countess Hoyos (neé Whitehead) whom Strutt considered a tiresome woman and who, in Strutt's opinion, was not very British in her views despite her nationality. Over a drink and a cigarette, Princess Lonyay startled them both with the news that three days before, her daughter, Princess Windisch- Gratz, had rung her crying that Red Guards were invading her house. As the house was just three doors down the road, she immediately ran over and told the swine that she and her daughter were cousins of King George of England and if they didn't clear out; she would send for Colonel Strutt!

Strutt was dismayed and responded with a horrified laugh. Countess Lonyay had made him into a bogey man. He would now be forced to fight battalions single-handed. He told her his death would be upon her head. She ignored him. The so-called Red Guards were so frightened at the aspect of encountering Strutt, they apologised and hurried off, warning her that they would return, but of course they hadn't. She turned fully to Strutt and said 'My dear Colonel, after that punctured tyre incident last week, you must understand your name is a force to be reckoned with!'

Strutt was very taken by this story which he had heard something about, but never with reference to himself, and he praised her for her courage. The whole thing could have ended very badly for her. Openly he praised her, but privately, he wondered if his new found reputation would turn out to be useful or just plain dangerous. He had hoped to stay under cover until he had made a plan.

As they tucked into their lunch, Strutt was agreeably surprised to find there was plenty of it. The day before, Princess Lonyay had brought up a collection of cold meats and vegetables and a strange-looking fruit cake from the Windisch-Gratz estate. Strutt considered her a lucky woman. Whatever happened in the future, her money being Belgian, would probably keep the Austrian estate secure.

After lunch, he popped by to see Maritschy Czernin. They had a long talk before the fire in her sitting room. He wanted to know why the Empress was so unpopular. It puzzled him. He had heard odd comments on all sides. He couldn't conceive how anyone could dislike her.

Maritschy shrugged. The trouble was that the people didn't know her. They believed it was all Zita's fault that they had lost the war because she was 'a foreigner'. They called her 'the Italian' and said she was never pro-Entente. They say she persuaded a weak Emperor to sue for peace behind Germany's back to suit the needs of her family. Maritschy knew it was unfair, ridiculous even. If anyone were to ask the Empress what her own nationality was, she would tell you she was international. Her father considered himself a Frenchman. They had homes in Austria, France, and Italy. The Sixtus Affair was a bad idea though, for her, the country and especially for Kary Czernin.

While she was speaking, Strutt remembered that the House of Bourbon-Parma was a cadet branch of the Spanish royal family. They once ruled as Kings of Etruria in France and as of Dukes of Parma, Piacenzo. Guastelle and Lucca in Italy. Zita's father was Robert I, last reigning Duke of Parma until 1859 when the duchy was absorbed into the new reunified Italian State. Zita's mother was a Braganza of the Portuguese ruling house. Her grandmother was French. Yes, Zita could well claim to be international.

Maritschy took a deep breath and held back tears, she was so worried about the future. They really must leave the country. She leaned closer and lowered her voice to a whisper. 'Kary has written to the Swiss to ask for refuge and they have refused him.' Seeing Strutt's grimace, she sat back.

She and Kary were such dear friends, he hated not to be able to promise her assistance. He could promise to do all in his power, but she must understand that at the moment, he did not see his own way clearly. She must have realised that he was sent to Austria to do an impossible job. If he failed, no one would come to his aid. He smiled at her. Had she not considered that he might end up worse off than she and Kary? He might be looking to them for help! Maritschy's eyes grew round, she had not thought of that. Looking up at him now, she realized how much he had changed. He was still handsome, still kind, but his hair was greying and between his dark eyes were deep creases of concentration. For the first time she realized he truly might not be able to help them.

Privately, it was becoming clear to Strutt that the Habsburgs would have to leave Austria, but he had no idea how this might come about. There was still a bit of time, so he told Maritschy she should keep calm. It could do Kary no good having her fussing all over him, he was probably worried enough for the two of them. Sadly, she agreed he was right and promised to try.

He left her then and drove back to Eckartsau feeling sad for them. He was upset for the millions of innocent people who had got caught up by and been smashed by the damnable war. Most of all, he was depressed by his own predicament, what the hell was he going to do now?

Chapter Twenty

March 17, 1919
The First Plan of Escape

It was a cold sunny afternoon, finding no one to walk with, Strutt went for a stroll along the Danube and found the Emperor sunning himself on a favourite rock. He waved to Strutt to join him. When he got within hearing distance, Karl told him the newspapers were commenting very rudely on him for having recently awarded the Order of the Gold Fleece to two or three distinguished people. It was outrageous! What had they to say to anything? Strutt said he'd heard nothing about it.

Karl then told him he'd done it on purpose, of course, to prove that he was still Emperor and could still do so. Why shouldn't he? Who was to stop him? He reminded Strutt that he had not abdicated, merely retired until the country quieted down. Strutt saw plainly the Emperor was in a snit and sat down ready to listen.

After a while during which the Emperor's mind wandered to a different subject, he proceeded to tell Strutt that the escutcheons of distinguished Englishmen who had received high Austrian decorations were still hanging in the Stefanskirche, the famous cathedral in Vienna. Did he know that? He assumed that King George had taken no action regarding those of the Austrian in St George's Chapel at Windsor.

Strutt had to tell him as tactfully as possible that the insignia of all Germans had been removed, of course, but that he was quite ignorant as to what had happened to those of other enemy nationalities. He discovered later that in fact, all foreign flags had been removed, but not the brass plates which were kept for historical reasons. The Emperor seemed mollified by this, but clearly still unhappy. When he rose to return to the Castle, Strutt thought it expedient to join him.

Just after lunch, a British Embassy car arrived with a very alarming telegram for Strutt from the War Office via Cuninghame. The message told him that the situation was such that it was highly advisable that he get the Emperor out of Austria at once and into Switzerland, but that 'the British Government can in no way guarantee your journey.' Strutt immediately asked for the Daimler and keeping his mouth firmly shut, left for Vienna.

Luckily, Cuninghame had just returned that morning from Prague and was in the Embassy. Strutt told him that his information on the ground pointed to the situation in Vienna being rather easier now, not worse. Cuninghame countered that he was wrong and not to underestimate Renner, who was shortly to be named Chancellor of the Austrian Republic.

So it was true that a Republic was going to be announced soon? Cuninghame told them they hadn't yet set a date, but he believed it would be soon. He smiled wolfishly at Strutt. The Knight Errant would have to think hard now, wouldn't he? Strutt curled his lip.

Cuninghame relaxed in his chair and presented Strutt with his gloomy opinion. His guess was that Renner would present the Emperor with three choices. First, if he would abdicate all rights, properties, perhaps a large portion of his wealth, he might be permitted to stay in Austria as a private citizen, but Cuninghame wouldn't trust that. Second, if the Emperor were to abdicate the throne, but not give up his rights, he would have to go immediately into exile. Third, if he refused to abdicate, he would almost certainly be interred at once under heavy guard.

After thinking it through, Strutt asked Cuninghame what he thought the Emperor's best choice should be? Despite his dislike of the man, he thought it useful to have his opinion. Cuninghame, after all, had been in Vienna for the better part of a year. He didn't expect Cuninghame's snide reply: 'This is your show, old chap. Figure it out yourself.'

Strutt's eyebrows came down in contempt, he knew Cuninghame hated him. He could bear that quite cheerfully, but he was disappointed at his prejudiced view of the Imperial Couple. All Cuninghame could see was that the Royals had once been the enemy. He has not taken on board that his Majesty had done his best, young as he was, to stop the war when he came to power; that he was as much a victim of the whole catastrophe as anyone else! Strutt slammed his crop down on the desk, turned and left the office. He now knew what he had to do.

He walked around to the Swiss legation, but it was closed. He then returned to the Embassy and sent for Lt Parker whom he had not seen since they travelled to Vienna from Fiume. Whatever his mission had been, he had succeeded. Nicolson had spoken well of him. Strutt wanted him to accompany him to the railway station to make some arrangements. Parker, who was at loose ends by then, was happy to help.

In a very short time they had arranged for a special train: one engine, one carriage and a van to be on standby at the West Bahnhof station, Vienna at 19.00 the following night. Parker was to make sure of its arrival and readiness on receipt of a message from Strutt by telephone later that evening saying 'Act'. Two British policemen would be on the train, making four of them altogether with Ashmore.

He then went back to the Swiss Legation and asked for the Minister, Monsieur Burckhardt, but he was away at Berne. Nevertheless, Strutt was received by the minister's son, a most charming and capable young man. Strutt told him quite frankly, but briefly what his intentions were and asked him whether his government would receive the Emperor. Young Burckhardt replied that he was not at all sure, as when the question was first put to them in November 1918, they had refused, but he would send a cipher message to Berne at once. He paused significantly.

'We have reason to believe that our cipher is not a hundred per cent reliable, Colonel. Do you still want me to try?'

Strutt gave this some thought. If he didn't take the risk, the Emperor would be trapped in the Republic which was to be announced any day. He decided to take Burckhardt fully into his confidence. He was going to bring the Emperor out in a British uniform in a special train to Buchs in Switzerland. The Allies had the right to commandeer trains. He would leave the Emperor there and then return to fetch out the rest of the Imperial Family. Could Burckhardt promise that the Swiss would not return the Emperor to Austria and intern Strutt? After some thought, Burckhardt thought he could and they parted the best of friends.

When Strutt got back to Eckartsau at about 21.00, he went straight to the Emperor. Count Esterhazy was on duty and went in to alert the Emperor of Strutt's presence. It was late, but of course, he would be received. The Emperor was in bed, comfortably propped up by pillows. Strutt went straight in.

He was sorry to disturb his Majesty at this late hour, but time was pressing. He paused to take a deep breath. This frail young man, lying on lace-trimmed pillows was going to have to take it straight. The unfortunate fact was that His Majesty was in grave danger of being arrested by the Provisional Government. They must act immediately. He then laid out for the Emperor the choices he thought Herr Renner would most likely offer him. By the end of this recital, the Emperor looked thoughtful. He couldn't believe it.

Was Strutt really sure of all this? It wasn't possible that anyone would act to arrest him. Strutt told him that in this new world, it was possible. It was imperative that they act now, he then explained to his Majesty what he had arranged.

Tomorrow night a train would be waiting for the two of them at West Bahnhof Station to take them to Buch. There should be no trouble. His Majesty would shave off his moustache, wear Strutt's spare uniform and take only one bag and one servant. Nobody would recognise him. Strutt would be with him on the train, but they would sit separately. Once at Buchs, Strutt would go back immediately for the rest of the family.

At this point, hearing voices, the Empress came in. Her black hair was done up in a long braid down her back. She looked a young girl in her fetching dressing gown. Seeing her, the Emperor asked that he leave them for the moment so that he could talk to her alone. Strutt thought his plan dished.

At 22.30, the Emperor sent for Strutt again when he was alone and said he would not go. Strutt was angry and made one more effort. If he must, he said, if the Emperor refused to leave, then he would take him by force! For a moment he thought the Emperor would yield, but then he shook his head and said 'Colonel, I cannot leave my wife and children.' How could he be seen to save only himself? He would be the biggest coward in the world.

Strutt was frustrated. How could he make the Emperor leave alone? There was no way to get the whole family secretly across Vienna to the West Bahnhof station. They would be recognised at the station, even if their car passed unnoticed beforehand. Strutt sympathized with the Emperor, but thought his scruples unnecessary. He hadn't yet figured out how to get the rest of the family out, but he knew he would find a way. He gave a tired sigh, clearly, he would have to come up with another plan.

Once out in the corridor, wanting confirmation of his own assessment, Strutt asked Herr Schager and Lt von Seedak, who were waiting there, if they thought there was any possibility that the people would welcome the Emperor back in power? They looked dubious.

Shonta thought not. The people wanted a new kind of government, one they could rule themselves. Schager agreed. 'The people have lost their faith in the idea of Empire,' he said. Well, thought Strutt, that decided that.

He hardly slept that night trying to find a solution. After breakfast, he went back to Vienna to the Swiss Legation. Young Burckhardt was beaming. The Swiss would receive the whole Imperial Family if the worst came to the worst! That was a relief. Strutt ruminated quietly that it was just like the Foreign Office to tell him to take the Habsburgs to Switzerland without first finding out if the Swiss would have them! He later reflected that, of course, they couldn't.

Food shortages in Vienna had now become acute. All the restaurants had closed, and the hotels were only feeding residents. He went around to the Embassy to pick up a large parcel of food that had arrived for him through the diplomatic bag. It was from Florrie, in the accompanying letter she told him to deliver the parcel to the Czernins. She was worried about them, Strutt knew she and Maritschy were the greatest of friends, so he immediately went round to their house and was delighted to discover there was another note in the parcel telling Maritschy to give Bill a good meal which Maritschy did with enormous pleasure.

While they were all enjoying a splendid lunch, Kary told him very seriously that with every hour the situation was getting worse. He needed to bolt across the frontier at once with his charges. Strutt well understood that although he had said little about his reason for being in Vienna, most of his friends had fathomed what it must be. Nevertheless, he was not yet ready to acknowledge it, so after dinner he left them pretending there was nothing to worry about for the present.

He then went on to Count Esterhazy's flat where Hunyady, Mensdorff, Count Kinsky, Schager and Countess Bellegarde were gathered over tea. All the men there also told him he ought to go as soon as possible. Only the Countess spoke to the contrary, her face flushed as she put both hands into her hair.

She disagreed, the Empress strongly believed they should stand and fight. She thought the people would rally to them if they showed some real courage now and stood their ground. Strutt smiled approval at her.

What a splendid girl the Empress was, he thought – game for anything, but in this she was wrong.

He, Gabriella Bellegarde and Hunyady, returned in the Daimler to Eckartsau at about 19.30. He enjoyed talking to them. Gabrielle was intelligent, forthright and brave. Hunyady was very similar, but in a more thoughtful and quiet way. They had got to know each other over the last few days. Zita had chosen her ladies-in-waiting well, he thought. In fact, he realised in a flash of insight, they were more like Staff Officers in disguise than social secretaries. His respect for Zita went up another notch. What a woman.

The next afternoon, when he and Gabriella returned from a seven mile walk, tired and dishevelled but happy, they ran into Zita coming back from the nursery. She was wearing a pale lavender wool dress which became her wonderfully. She asked them brightly if they had enjoyed their walk and where had they gone this time? Strutt detected some annoyance in her tone.

Gabriella told her with some elation that they had got almost to Pavli. It was quite a climb. The Colonel had to pull her up the last mile. Bantering with her, Strutt laughed. She would never be a mountain climber if she thought that road was steep. It was as flat as his hand. Laughing into Zita's eyes, Gabriella told her not to believe him. It was a mountain!

The Empress' reaction surprised them both. Rather coolly, she asked if the Countess had remembered to finish ordering the supplies for the end of the week. When receiving a startled reply from Gabriella in the affirmative, she then told her that Count Hunyady had been asking for her. You might go and find him.

Gabriella knew a dismissal when she heard one and was intrigued. The Empress was obviously jealous of her time with the Colonel. When had that last happened, she wondered? Not since they were at school together, she was sure. She turned to Strutt and told him she would ignore his insults about her climbing fitness and thanked him for escorting her this afternoon, it had been fun. She would see them both at dinner.

When she was gone, Strutt gave Zita a long look. Where did this reserve suddenly come from? She stood a few feet before him with her eyes on her hands. Zita was feeling ashamed of being rude to her dearest friend. She was confused by her feelings and fighting an overwhelming urge to put her head on the Colonel's shoulder. She had been strong for so long. He would comfort her and tell her everything would be all right.

Strutt broke the silence and softly told her she could have gone with them if she had wanted to. She would have been welcome. She looked into his deep warm eyes and knew he understood. She blushed. She was being silly, wasn't she?

Strutt told her that a woman like her could never be anything less than honest and true. Like anyone, she might become confused before the full facts were known. Who doesn't? But when all was known, she would always point due North, like a compass. Zita smiled, still not looking at him. She was, after all, still in her twenties. She was not a compass, she said, just a small female caught up in events she couldn't control.

Strutt smiled and sought to put her at ease. She was doing a splendid job, he said. He didn't know any officer of his acquaintance who could have managed better than she had in these circumstances. If she were a soldier, he told her, she would without a doubt have won several medals by now. His eyes were warm and kind.

Hearing this stirring praise, Zita looked up and beamed. Coming from him, she considered that an enormous compliment. She squared her shoulders, she would immediately stop worrying. They would find a way out of their current impasse. She knew it. Feeling greatly cheered by his comments, she left him, throwing a sweet smile over her shoulder.

Strutt watched her stroll briskly down the corridor. This woman was a marvel – discreet, attractive, fecund to a ridiculous degree and so very courageous and capable. If things were different, he would have given her the encouraging hug she obviously needed, but she was an Empress. He went up to bathe and change.

Chapter Twenty-One

March 17, 1919
A Theft and a Confrontation

An hour later, Ashmore came rushing in to find him. One of their food wagons had been attacked on its way to the castle. What food wagons? Strutt was buttoning his cufflinks. He thought the British Mission supplied all their foodstuffs.

Ashmore said that was correct for the most part, but it seemed the Empress still relied on two or three local farms for fresh vegetables and milk. Count Hunyady wanted his opinion downstairs. Could he come right away?

Within half an hour, Strutt, Ashmore, Shonta and Hunyady had driven off down the road to the place where a large-framed wagon was turned over and found empty. A boy was gentling the horses after removing their traces. The peasant driver, dressed in old boots and a long worn jacket and sheepskin hat was sitting by the roadside a picture of utter defeat. He glanced up with Strutt's party appeared. Shonta talked to him and Hunyady translated.

> 'He says he was on his way to deliver the produce to the royal kitchen as usual, when six Austrian soldiers forced him to stop and get down from the wagon. They said it was illegal to sell produce anymore to the Imperial Family and they were taking it for their own needs.'

Strutt wanted to know if there was an army camp around them somewhere. He hadn't seen one in his walks. Shonta said there wasn't. It was conceivable, however, that a group of Republican soldiers might have come out from Vienna to make life even more difficult for them. The driver had also told them the officer had given him what he said was a receipt for the goods they took. How extraordinary! He handed Strutt a sealed envelope addressed to Herr Karl Habsburg.

Since when do thieves hand out receipts, wondered Strutt as he opened the letter which contained not one but two pages. The first was a receipt for the vegetables and other goods. The other was a disgustingly obscene letter written to the Empress telling her that no more supplies would be forthcoming. Both pages were signed Ober Leutnant S. Muller. Strutt saw red.

In a fury, he asked Shonta to ask the driver if he knew who this Leutnant Muller was. Shonta immediately did so. The driver scratched his beard and told Shonta the officer had said 'the Colonel would remember him from the train last week.'

Strutt's memory instantly threw up a picture of the sneering officer on the train. So, he thought with steely resolve, now we know your name, you blackguard. He put the envelope carefully into his tunic and told the others it really was a receipt. It looked like Austrian soldiers stationed in Vienna did feel emboldened to come out here and do as they liked. Whether or not they were Bolsheviks, it was hard to say. Did it matter? This whole development was not a good sign.

A coldness had come over Strutt like it did before battle. His Empress had been insulted by a swine of an Austrian officer turned republican; a man so sure of a republican victory and the downfall of the Habsburgs, that he wasn't afraid to sign his own name. This was real danger. 'Come on', he said to the others. 'We're going back to the castle and this time I'm going to have it out with the head of the family!'

Back at Eckartsau, Strutt knocked rapidly on the door to Zita's office. There was no time to waste. Gabriella let him in, her eyebrows raised. Both she and the Empress had been working at their desks by the windows. The room was chilly. To save firewood, it was their custom not to light the fire until tea time at 4.00. Both ladies were consequently wrapped up in shawls. Strutt came straight to the point when the Empress walked forward to greet him with questioning eyes.

In a rush, he told her time was no longer on their side. One of the wagons that supplied the kitchens was attacked that morning, probably by republican soldiers. Who knew who else was out there? How many of them? The castle could not be defended and he could not answer for their safety if they continued to remain there.

Zita was steady as she searched his face. Could this really be true? He told her it was. He had never been surer of anything in his life.

The Empress took a turn around the room. When she came back to face him, she stood tall and looked him in the eye with great conviction. She and the Emperor could never run away. These were their people. Strutt admired her for this, but he was unmoved.

Bracing himself to be cruel, he told her that he had heard from all sides that the people didn't want a monarchy anymore. They didn't want them! He hated to tell her this, but it was the truth. The people think they can rule themselves better in the future. Worse, he was told that Budapest was in revolt and Linz and Salzburg were little better. Republican soldiers, Bolsheviks and hundreds of angry deserters were wandering the countryside – right now!

While she listened intently to this shocking news, Zita held her ground. She told him the Emperor would never abdicate and she would never ask him to. He would never leave without her and she would not leave without the children, so they were stuck there, were they not?

Strutt was exasperated. This was not a chess game, this was real life. They must leave or they were in danger of dying here. Look at what happened to the Romanovs. At this, Zita turned white. Seeing her weaken, he told her one day they might come back if the people changed their minds. One day they might have a choice!

Zita looked daggers at him and told him he was forgetting himself! She was now very angry and her eyes flashed. Did he think she would allow the Emperor to give up so easily? Yes, they were in difficulties at the moment and they were grateful for his help, but Habsburgs had ruled these lands for over six hundred years. As a family, they were Austria-Hungary. They held a sacred trust from the people which they would never relinquish.

She paused and walked around the room again. She knew all about losing thrones. Her family, the Bourbon-Parmas, had been thrown out of two kingdoms. They had ruled in Italy and also in France. She knew what defeat was. The Emperor didn't. His grandfather, Franz Joseph, had held off a revolution in 1848 and they would, too. With strong leadership, the people *would* support them.

Finally, seeing her stubbornness, Strutt raised his voice. The time for all that was past! They had no army, no support whatsoever in government. A dead Habsburg was no good to anyone, whereas a live one with a family, might yet succeed. She bridled at this and tears formed in her lovely eyes. He took her hands in his and gently entreated her. There might well come a time when the people would want them again. If they went now, they had a chance, didn't she see?

After this onslaught, Zita pulled herself together and paused to wipe her eyes. Finally, she clasped her hands before her with a sigh, bowed her head and with a voice grown husky she agreed to do as he asked. She would do all she could to help him.

The tone of this interview had started out fairly rationally, but it increasingly had become emotional for both of them. Strutt cared very much what happened to Zita on a personal level and she knew it. In the background, the forgotten Countess Bellegarde coughed.

Strutt left Zita's room and went up to his own to calm down and decided what must be done. He would let the Empress first talk things over with the Emperor. She must make him understand that they had to go and soon. He figured Karl would agree to anything Zita suggested. She might even come up with a serviceable plan. He stayed in his room until dinner time.

Chapter Twenty-Two

March 17-19, 1919
First Meeting with Karl Renner

After dinner, Count Hunyady said the Emperor would be grateful if he would join him in his private room. Strolling down the corridors, Strutt was pleased to see the light bulbs had been replaced. Hunyady told him it had been a major effort to find enough. Herr Schager was waiting outside the Emperor's door and went in with them.

The Emperor was in bed and had been thinking things over now that Zita had persuaded him they must leave. He truly did not want to leave the country, but he understood they were no longer safe there. What would they think of the idea of removing to his castle at Innsbruck? He had been told it was in an Allied occupied zone. Did they think they would be safe there?

Strutt grimaced. He doubted it. The authorities there were all Italian revolutionaries. He did not think they would agree to receive him. The Emperor rather peevishly thought there were British troops there. Strutt had to correct him. British troops were to the west at Imst.

The four men considered other ideas, but nothing seemed to work. In the end, Strutt reluctantly said he would go the next day and ask Renner, the Secretary of State for the Provisional Government, if Innsbruck would accept the Emperor in their area. Strutt turned his head and saw Zita had opened the door a crack and had been listening to their conversation. She called softly to her husband and came in. The meeting was over.

Strutt found time a few days later to remark in his diary that no more affectionate and devoted a couple could be found than Zita and the Emperor. Despite the huge difference in their characters, or maybe because of it, they truly loved each other; Zita with her deep reservoir of strength and intellect and Karl with his enormous warmth and kindness. He loved his people and had really tried to do well by them. You couldn't help but like him, despite his many failings. Strutt wrote 'the gutter press in Austria and Germany must recoil on their own front pages from all the lies they tell about the Imperial Couple.' It was a disgusting state of affairs.

The next day, Strutt arrived at the Embassy in Vienna just in time to find that Nicholson, the cipher expert, was about to leave for Prague again. In some distress, Nicholson said he was truly sorry to leave him at this juncture, when everything was looking so bad for the Imperial Family. It would mean he was cut off from London.

Strutt told him he was already cut off, so not to worry. Nicholson then gave him another message from the Foreign Office via Colonel Cuninghame. He read it out loud to Nicholson:

The Austrian Government now wants the Emperor to leave Austria. Every facility should be afforded to the Emperor by Strutt to reach the Swiss frontier in safety should he wish to go there, although the British Government cannot guarantee the journey.

Strutt snorted. So the Austrians wanted the Emperor to go and he was to help him, but the British Government would deny all knowledge of it if it all went belly up. Well he knew that already, didn't he? Nightmares always got worse.

Nicholson was distressed. He was very sorry, but there was more and he gave Strutt a copy of the *Arbeiter Zeitung*, a low class rag of a newspaper which claimed the Emperor was running away to Switzerland after asking for asylum. There was an article in it which also reported the wagon incident the previous day showing the Emperor in a very poor light. Strutt started to swear – in German.

After listening to these fulminations, Nicholson was almost wringing his hands with worry. He was incredibly sorry, but he must leave at once if he was to catch the 14.30 train to Prague and he wasn't sure when he would be back. He was very afraid Strutt would be on his own. Then he paused tentatively and asked if Strutt might like to give him his wife's address? Strutt, startled, barked out a laugh.

'What?! For God's sake man, it's not as bad as all that.' Nicholson did not look relieved, but tried to smile anyway. 'But thanks for the offer.' The two men shook hands and took their leave. Strutt went away impressed by young Nicholson. Capability and kindness were not characteristics that went together very often in his experience. He hoped he might see him again.

An hour later, Strutt arrived at Renner's office, which was located in the very ornate town hall. It was one of the distinguished buildings put up in the last century to house government departments. It looked shabby now due to lack of maintenance. He was not kept waiting long before he was shown into Renner's office and announced. Renner, bald and bespectacled, with sharp waxed moustaches and a goatee, was sitting alone at small conference table. He did not get up to greet him.

Thanks to Yella Szechenyi, he knew something of Karl Renner's lowly background. That he had risen to high office from such a humble start was to his credit. He was waiting to see what his own opinion of the man might be. Renner didn't move. He just stared at Strutt from his seat at the table.

'You will stand up in future when a British Officer enters your room!' Strutt shouted at him in fluent German. Renner, shocked by the electric force of Strutt's personality, sprang up at once, twitching his hands. Strutt then sat at the table and graciously invited Renner to join him. He noticed out of the corner of his eye that a door leading to the adjoining office was ajar and moved every now and then. Other officials obviously knew he was here and had come to listen.

> 'I have come on the Emperor's behalf to demand that you instantly deny the statement made in the press yesterday that the Emperor has asked the Swiss to receive him. You inferred that the Emperor is running away. He would never do that! He would never leave his family to save himself. It is an infamous slander to say otherwise and you will say that I, Colonel Strutt say so.'

Renner was cringing. He assured Strutt that he had nothing whatsoever to do with the article and would, of course, tell the editor of his interest. Renner got up to reach for the telephone.

Strutt told him to sit down. This would not do. He, Strutt, would dictate to him the new article that will appear in the morning's newspaper. Renner at once agreed and Strutt dictated the statement.

While Renner was in the middle of writing, the 'three scoundrels', as Strutt called them, all members of the new government, entered the room from the moving door and were introduced as Herren Klein, Seitz and Deutsch. Strutt suspected that Otto Bauer, the current Minister of Foreign Affairs, was still hiding behind the door. He proceeded to bawl them all out for not seeing that the Emperor and his household were properly supplied with food and fuel. They all apologised for the wagon incident.

Strutt then pulled out the obscene letter to Herr Karl von Habsburg and showed it to them. Not one of them made any comment. Strutt then scolded them in a soft, terrifying voice.

'You have nothing to say to this outrage, this insult to your Empress – a woman of the highest integrity and nobility of spirit; a woman worth more than a thousand of you?' All four men stared at the floor in frightened silence. Strutt calmed himself and asked Renner for a private conversation. Shaken, the three other men left the room.

Then, sitting back comfortably in his chair, Strutt fixed Renner with a limpid eye and told him that he was thinking of moving the Imperial Family from Eckartsau, as the neighbourhood did not seem to be under any sort of control anymore.

Renner, nervously eager to placate Strutt, told him that his resources were limited, but he would be happy to facilitate any move the Emperor desired to make. His Majesty must know that the Republic was shortly to be announced.

Strutt ignored the reference to the Republic. He was thinking of removing the Imperial Family to Innsbruck. They have a house there, but he wasn't entirely sure of the security situation there. Could Renner help?

Renner was all eagerness. He would ring the Tyrolese officials that afternoon and see if they would accept the Imperial Family. He then looked defensive. 'You do understand, Colonel. That I have no authority there? I can but inquire on his Majesty's behalf.'

They arranged that one of Renner's staff would telephone the words YES or NO at exactly 22.00 that night to Strutt at Eckartsau. He would do it without fail. Strutt considered the chances of this and satisfied, rose from his chair. Renner accompanied him to the street with a shower of assurances, bowed in fawning fashion and Strutt departed.

Once back at the castle in the evening, Strutt went at once to visit the Emperor who looked very depressed at his news. He didn't really want to go anywhere, as he was not well again. Strutt was merciless. He told him Renner had said Austria would be declared a Republic in five days time. He had no choice but to leave the country for his own safety and that of his family.

'Promise me that I shall leave as Emperor and not as a thief in the night', the Emperor cried weakly from his pillows. Strutt promised with some hesitation. He would try at least. The Emperor was pale with worry. Strutt felt the shock of seeing such a young man looking so frail. He softened his voice and told him not to worry and get some sleep. All would be well.

As Strutt entered the corridor, the Empress came out of her room to tell him she was arranging that they would go to Wartegg near Rorschach on Lake Constance to stay with her Mother, the Duchess of Parma. She had written telegrams in code for him to send. He was flabbergasted. This was a far better solution than the castle at Innsbruck. Zita was well ahead of the game and he congratulated her warmly, admiration glowing in his eyes. As it was late in the evening, she was wearing a long, lilac wool tea gown with a very pretty white lace shawl over it.

She looked rather adorable, in fact, but flustered as well. He realised she wanted to ask him something, so he gave her an opening. Looking at the wall, the Empress lightly asked him if Queen Marie had begged him for all sorts of favours. She expected she had. Strutt wondered if she had started to feel guilty about all he was doing for them and replied 'Not for herself, no. But she did ask me whether I thought her daughter had a chance of marrying the Prince of Wales.' Zita was incredulous.

'Well, that's one thing you needn't fear I will ask you, Colonel!' She laughed up at him. Strutt looked at her with tenderness. He took her hand and bowed over it. She could ask him for anything, she must know that. His eyes met hers and the Empress blushed, fluttered her hand and withdrew back to her room, wishing him good night as she shut the door. Whatever she had wanted to ask him, he thought, it would have to wait.

Chapter Twenty-Three

March 20, 1919
The Second Plan of Escape

Needless to say, Renner did not ring at 22.00 as promised, so Strutt rang him. He got his staff instead. The answer to whether the Tyrolean officials would allow the Imperial Family refuge was a resounding NO. Strutt was not surprised, as he had expected this would be the case.

The next morning, he went to Vienna early to talk to the Food Commission people. Mr Butler, the Commissioner, was there. When Strutt told him of his plan, he understood immediately and promised he would deal with it personally. Time was pressing.

Strutt then went to the railway station to talk to the Station Master, an intelligent middle-aged man with clear grey eyes. Strutt informed him, as he no doubt already knew, that as a Senior British Officer, Strutt had the power to commandeer a train. The Station Master had been told no such thing, but in this instance, looking at Strutt's fierce and haughty demeanour, he decided not to dispute the issue. Strutt then proceeded to order a special train ostensibly for the British Food Commission to be ready the day after tomorrow. He gave the Station Master a detailed list of the number of carriages and wagons required, along with a shorter list of items that would be needed to make it safe and comfortable. The Station Master now had a good idea for whom the train was being readied and an even bigger reason to not ask any questions. 'All will be as you have requested, Excellenz,' was all he said.

Strutt then went to see the train schedulers to discuss the route. They were not happy about some of his plans and recommended alternatives, but it soon became clear that Strutt knew the timetables and routes as well as they did. More importantly, he also knew where trouble might lie along the way. He chose the safest routes even when that meant a longer journey.

When everything was organised, he went back to see Renner, who sprang to his feet immediately Strutt came within sight. It had been a busy morning. Renner would be happy to hear that Strutt had ordered a train to take the Imperial Family to Switzerland. Renner was not happy at all, he felt offended that Strutt had effected so much in a short time, but this feeling was quickly overshadowed by relief. Bringing his hand to his chest, he assured Strutt that his government had no wish that any harm should come to the Imperial Family. They knew full well the entire Entente would come down on their necks. No, he would make it his personal responsibility to see there would be no trouble, but, of course there would be one or two requirements.

Strutt stilled. He asked Renner what those requirements might be. The bald man, slightly trembling in the menacing force that rolled off the quiet Strutt, replied that the luggage would have to be searched. Strutt refused. And, continued Renner, a High Commissioner would have to travel on the train with them to make sure no regrettable incidents occurred.

Strutt looked Renner straight in the eye and promised to shoot any High Commissioner should anything go wrong. He did agree, however, that the Emperor would take away nothing that was not his personal property. This was a safe bet, he thought, given the vast amount the Emperor owned.

At this point Otto Bauer entered the room and asked Renner for an introduction. This was the Minister of Foreign Affairs who almost certainly had been hiding behind the door yesterday and probably this morning as well. Strutt was not impressed. He was a little man with disproportionate mustachios.

Bauer, as Strutt had learned from dearest Yella and others, was once a lieutenant in the Austrian Army, but in 1916 he deserted to the Russians who immediately arrested him as an enemy spy. In the POW camp, he became so enamoured of Bolshevism the authorities decided in 1918 that he would be of more use to them back in Austria. They let him go. He rejoined the Social Democratic Party and became the leader of its left wing. His goal appeared to be unification with Germany, not wholesale revolution, but like most of his ilk, in Strutt's experience, self-advancement was the primary motivation.

Bauer, having overheard the conversation with Renner, was very cordial as he confirmed that all would be as Strutt requested. Strutt bowed very slightly, wished them both a good day and left. He wasn't fooled. Bauer looked to him like the lowest sort of thief, which meant his word was worthless. He knew exactly what to expect from both of them -betrayal. They were making his task too easy.

That night at dinner, Strutt sent up a note requesting a meeting afterwards with the Empress and her two ladies in waiting in her private sitting room. The castle was very quiet as he walked down the hall to her apartments. The three women, all resolved to do whatever was necessary, had asked Count Hunyady to join them. He rose when Strutt appeared and said he would leave if Strutt preferred. Strutt apologised for not sending for him in the first place and indicated that he should sit down again. He himself paced the room.

Finally he faced them with his hands behind his back and told them the plans he had made on their behalf. In four days time, Austria would be declared a Republic and none of them would be safe after that. The Emperor had refused to leave without his family, therefore they must all leave with him. He had arranged for a train which would accommodate the family, a few of the Court and some servants. It would leave from Kopfsetten, the nearest station to the castle at 19.00 on Sunday.

All four of his listeners gasped. So soon? Hunyady sat forward in his chair thinking hard. Two days was not much time to pack up. Also, how were they to select who would accompany the Imperial Family? This was going to take formidable organisation. He took Gabriella's hand and squeezed it. They would do it. Gabriella looked at him admiringly. They had decided to be married in May regardless of circumstances and she was glad.

Meanwhile, the Empress hadn't moved, but she had made some decisions. They would need lorries to move the luggage to the train. Had the Colonel asked for flat cars to transport their two best automobiles? They would no doubt need them in Switzerland. Gabriella could see that all their valuables were packed. Agnes would deal with the family and servants and choose which to take with them. They would need to know approximately how many people the train could accommodate and make arrangements for the rest of the Court to find their own way home. Joseph, she said looking at Count Hunyady, could deal with that.

Little Countess Agnes Schoenborn spoke up. She would stay to make sure the rest of the Court got home. Some of them were elderly. They couldn't just abandon them. Zita said there was no question of that, but she hadn't yet thought of a plan for them. Agnes said she could leave all the arrangements to her. She would see to it and then rejoin her own family after that. Zita took her hand with great affection and thanked her. Agnes was so small and pretty and sweet, people never guessed how very capable she was, but Zita knew and was grateful. They could never have managed without her.

Strutt sat down at this point, grateful to have her take command. Zita was in full flood. Eyes flashing, her quick brain was conjuring up a full list of requirements for the coming two days. What a General she would have made! How could a woman, so young and small, have so much courage. He marvelled.

He then interrupted her to leave them to their planning. He had to go to Vienna first thing to make final arrangements, but would call on her in the afternoon. If any of them wanted a ride into town, he would be leaving at 9.00 in the morning.

Chapter Twenty-Four

March 21, 1919
The Bluff

Early the next morning, Saturday, the last day before leaving, Strutt rushed to Vienna with Ashmore and the two Countesses. He dropped them all off near the Ring so that they could make some last minute arrangements and Ashmore could take care of a little job for him. He then went around to the Railways Officer and confirmed the timetable. Then he went to the British Food Commission and made sure that two lorries would go out to Eckartsau for the luggage at 12.00 sharp the next day. Mr Butler assured him this would happen. The train would arrive at Kopfsetten at 15.45 on Sunday, which would give plenty of time to load up the luggage. They would all then depart at 19.00, two hours after dark. He was not leaving anything to chance.

While he was at the Commission, Renner telephoned and asked to see him at once. Strutt agreed and put down the telephone to muse for a moment. Had Renner remembered his three choices? It was too late to call off the plans now. What he needed was a clincher, a little insurance that Renner would not renege on the deal.

'Butler, old man, do you happen to have a blank telegraph form? I think I may need one.'

Butler invited him into his office, opened a couple of drawers in his desk and found the requisite form. He was curious to know what Strutt was up to. He had formed a deep respect for the man who was undertaking such a dangerous task.

Strutt wrote something on the form, folded it and put it carefully into his breast pocket. 'An insurance policy,' he said with a grim smile and thanked Butler for all his help. He hoped they might meet again in London one day.

Mr Butler wished him the best of British luck and the two shook hands.

Ashmore was waiting for him in the car. 'Did you get that address I asked you to find for me?' he asked. Ashmore, with a wary, but discreet expression, handed over a slip of paper. It was Leutnant Muller's office address. Strutt pocketed the paper and told the driver to take him to City Hall. 'You can come in with me.'

When Strutt entered Renner's office, with Ashmore in tow, Renner at once attacked him.

'You think you are so clever that you can take the Emperor away without an abdication! I told you my government will not allow him to leave unless he abdicates.'

'Really', replied Strutt with iron in his voice. 'Just what will you do? What can you do? After all, the Republic has not yet been declared. This is still a monarchy'.

Renner started to shout. 'I can intern him at once unless he abdicates! I can have you both interned!' He was not going to let Strutt out-manoeuvre him.

Strutt looked at him coldly for a whole minute. Ashmore was holding his breath. Then, taking a sheet of paper slowly from his breast pocket, he said 'I am very sorry to hear that, because if you even attempt to intern any of us, I will be forced to send this telegram.' He laid it on Renner's desk.

The telegram was addressed to the 'Directory of Military Intelligence – London' and it said:

As the Austrian Government refuses permission for the departure of Emperor unless he abdicates, the undersigned has issued orders to re-establish the blockade and to stop all supply trains coming into Austria as of this evening. (signed) Lt Colonel Edward Strutt.

Renner read the telegram and all bluster drained from him. He cringed back.

'Grosse Gott, you would starve the entire country?'

Strutt's coldness had turned to ice. 'Without a doubt.'

There was a short pause while Renner thought, and then conceded. 'All right. All right, he can go.'

'Without any conditions?'

'Yes, damn it. We will be glad to be rid of him!'

Strutt picked up the telegram and started to walk from the room, but Renner wasn't finished. He had been shocked into frankness.

'You know, Colonel, it is a great pity the British haven't sent troops into Austria.'

Strutt was exasperated. 'Yes, why is that?' he asked.

'Oh, because we like to see them walking about. They are always so smart and orderly,' he replied ingenuously.

Strutt snorted and turned on him. 'Because we're so smart and orderly?! Do you think me a fool? You'd like us to be here to save your dirty skin from the Bolsheviks who may well be here any minute! Your country doesn't count for you. Only your life and the lives of your few precious friends! Your Emperor trusted you by giving you high position and you thanked him by betraying him. I hope the Bolshies get you.'

This was hardly diplomatic fare, but Strutt couldn't help it. He left Renner leaning weakly against the window. Everything Strutt had said was true and he knew it.[1] Strutt and Ashmore left the building.

'Well done, sir!' said Ashmore in some awe as they walked down the stairs. 'You really scared him. Would you really have sent the telegram?'

Strutt gave him a cynical smile. 'Don't be silly, Ashmore. There is no Directory of Military Intelligence. It was a bluff.'

Strutt was pleased with himself as he left Ashmore standing with his mouth open. He directed him to meet him with the car back at the Embassy at 17.00 hours. That should fix Renner, he thought. It was less likely now that there would be any interference at Kopfstetten, but he knew it was a risk, a big one. They would have to take great care.

He walked around to lunch with Princess Festetic to rid his head of Renner's polluting presence. A group of his old friends had gathered there and greeted him warmly. Everyone was afraid of what was going to happen when the Republic was announced. Taszilo and his brother, George, had gone off to check on their Hungarian estates.

The dear old Princess Mary, her grey hair falling over her face, told him how worried she was about her husband. Taszilo was insistent on having his private train saloon, a sumptuous vehicle, attached to the daily Marchegg train of mixed goods wagons and bomb-damaged fourth class carriages.

---

1. Strutt considered Karl Renner, corrupt as he was, the only man of any capability in the government of German Austria at that time. Indeed, he survived to become President of Parliament in the National Council of Austria in 1931.

'I told him he would draw attention to himself and he would wind up being arrested!'

Strutt tried to reassure her, things weren't that bad yet. Privately, he thought he was mad. He then had a marvellous mental picture of a magnificent Taszilo mounting the steps of the guillotine, his powdered footman lining the way. He had to stifle a laugh.

All through the meal, a good one, friends muttered to him that "he must go.' He pretended not to hear. He didn't want anyone to know they were leaving the next day. After lunch, he briefly went around to the Esterhazy flat where there were many friends of the Imperial Family gathered, including Archduke Max and Count Hunyady. He wanted to say good bye to those who were in on the secret and they overwhelmed him with kindness.

Chapter Twenty-Five

March 21, 1919
Doing the Needful

After leaving the Festetics house just after 15.00, Strutt borrowed a car from the Embassy pool and drove to the back of the Food Commission where he knew non-commissioned ranks often gathered to chat and share a drink. In fact, there was usually a crowd of them there every day.

Ever since intercepting the obscene letter addressed to the Empress, he had quietly seethed that a depraved villain like Leutnant Muller should dare to throw muck at one of the three great Queens of the war.[1] It more than infuriated him, he felt it viscerally as a personal affront. In his gut, the Leutnant symbolised for him the random horror of the last five years; the nauseating evil of men unleashed from civilization.

His Empress was not just a great queen, she was the bravest woman he had ever met and moreover, she was under his protection. In another life, he admitted to himself, he might possibly have fallen in love with her, but that was an irrelevance here. In this life, she needed a champion. Her husband was incapable of fulfilling that role, no matter how much he loved her. Strutt had resolved to deal with the matter himself. His eyes narrowed.

When he arrived at the back of the Food Commission, he got out of the car and had a good look at the men gathered there before approaching a heavy-set Scottish sergeant who looked like he knew how to handle himself. He approached him and asked if he would mind doing a small job for him.

'Just a small job, Sergeant. A bit of a tidy-up exercise, actually. We'll be back in under an hour.'

---

1. The others, in Strutt's estimation, were Queen Elisabeth of the Belgians and Queen Marie of Romania.

'Right you are, sir.'

The two men got into Strutt's car and drove to the address Ashmore had found for him. It was a supply depot office on the outskirts of the city. Outside, there was a young Red Guard slouching on the steps smoking a cigarette. His rifle was between his knees.

The two men got out of the car. Strutt asked the guard in German where Ober Leutnant Muller could be found and pointedly waited for the man to get to his feet and hold open the door for them. The guard was uneasy at the look in Strutt's eye. The two men went inside the empty corridor and up the stairs to an office door. Strutt whispered to the Scottish sergeant to watch his back.

The surprised sergeant looked at Strutt with wide eyes. Clearly, something nasty was about to happen. He nodded. Strutt entered the office where Leutnant Muller was working at a desk.

'Good afternoon, Leutnant Muller,' he said in a quiet voice. Muller at once recognised him and rose to his feet.

'You!'

Strutt threw the obscene letter onto the desk. Had he written this? Muller snatched it up and sneered at him.

'What of it? They deserve all they get.'

'You think so?' Strutt's face turned menacing as he said this. Muller instantly put his hands up to fend him off.

'And what do you deserve, Leutnant, for insulting your Empress so foully? There is only one answer to that, don't you think?' Muller was frozen with fright by Strutt's terrifying eyes and before he could cry out, Strutt pulled his revolver from its case, shot the man dead and watched with satisfaction as his body slithered down the wall behind the desk. He then reholstered his gun, picked up the letter and rejoined the sergeant in the hallway. Startled by the shot, he too had drawn his gun.

'Job done, Sergeant. Let's go.' When the two men exited the warehouse, there was no soldier in evidence, just a rifle lying on the steps. Strutt kicked it away. Useless sod.

The drive back to the Food Commission didn't take long. He dropped the thoughtful sergeant near the crowd at the back door. 'This should do you, sergeant. Thank you for your help.'

The soldier looked at him and said in a thick Scottish accent. 'Any time, Colonel. I'm free most of tomorrow if ye want to fit in a few more little jobs...' 'I'll keep that in mind, sergeant,' Strutt drawled, giving him a half smile. The soldier got out of the car, saluted him ironically and Strutt drove on back to the Embassy and returned the borrowed car. He felt at peace.

As ordered, Ashmore was at the Embassy with the Daimler at 17.00 to collect him. Strutt got in and directed the driver to a smart residence where they collected the Countesses Bellegarde and Schoenborn.

'Thank you for coming for us, Colonel,' said Gabriella Bellegarde. We just wanted to see them one last time. We couldn't of course say goodbye.' The two ladies sat in the back together next to Strutt. Ashmore was in front with the driver.

They were all pensive, very aware this was the last time they would make this journey. It was still very cold for late March and they were glad for the fur rugs. Twilight came and the streets began to empty. Most people were inside in the warm, but on street corners a few men and women and miserable, starving children were left to huddle forlornly. It was a ghastly sight. Presently it began to snow. Strutt asked the driver to stop and he and Ashmore put the top up.

While the men were engaged, Gabriella whispered to Agnes. Would they ever return to Schoenbrunn?

Huddled in her furs, Agnes was quiet. After a while she sighed. It was unlikely. She was worried about travelling back to Vienna herself, but she wouldn't go alone. She asked Gabriella if she was really planning to go with the Imperial Family to Switzerland?

Gabriella whispered in her ear. 'Yes, but after that Joseph and I are thinking of bringing forward our marriage. After we see them to Switzerland, there will be little more we can do.' The two women exchanged a long look.

They were interrupted by Strutt getting back into the car in very good humour. He had decided to cheer them up with the tale of how he had routed Herr Renner that morning. They would be amused, he promised them.

After screaming with laughter at his amazing bluff and overcome once again by his courage, both countesses sobered and told Strutt that the Emperor and Empress must never be told how he secured their freedom. It would hurt them so much to know of the indignity.

Chapter Twenty-Six

March 23, 1919
The Last Day

It was Sunday, the last day. From 09.00 onward, people started arriving by car at Eckartsau. Strutt was furious. He had wanted complete anonymity, but it was impossible, he supposed grimly, to expect so many people to keep such a secret. The new arrivals were family members and old friends who had found safe billets in Vienna and the countryside. They clasped the Imperial Couple's hands and poured out encouragement and endless wishes for their safety and for a happy return when things 'got back to normal.' Strutt could see in their eyes that most of them feared they were saying goodbye for the last time. It was quite heart-rending, but Karl and Zita stood up well to it.

While all this was going on Strutt, Shonta and Ashmore were on the alert worrying about approaching danger. Word had come that a group of Bolsheviks were marauding just a few miles away and of course, there was the ever present worry that Renner would try to prevent them from leaving. At 10.00 there was Mass in the beautiful baroque chapel. It was crammed to suffocation. The Emperor and Empress were in the gallery. Little Archduke Otto served the Bishop.

Before the service, the organist played selections from Wagner, principally Parisfal and it was most affecting. At the end, the Austrian National Anthem was sung by all, perhaps for the last time in the presence of an Austrian Emperor. Everyone was sobbing, and Strutt felt a bit sentimental himself.

As the Imperial Family left the chapel, a number of villagers, all sad-eyed and often weeping, came up to say goodbye as well. Strutt was irritated by the crowds of people and said, with a snarl to Ashmore, 'So much for leaving in secret. We'll be lucky to get out here at all.'

During the night, he had realised there was nothing to stop Renner from changing his mind and having the train seized before they would get away. It wouldn't take much. Renner might even have thought of using the Emperor as a bargaining chip with the Bolsheviks. Hideous scenarios had rolled through his mind most of the night.

Ashmore came up to his shoulder and whispered, 'Do you see that man in the trees over there?' He nodded to a spot some distance away. Sure enough, Strutt saw a dark figure standing in the line of trees. He told Ashmore to get a couple of their policemen to go and have a look. It could be a poacher or just and interested bystander. No need to imagine the worst immediately.

There were several of Strutt's own friends among all the visitors who had come out from Vienna for the day to say farewell. One of them to his surprise was Countess Yella Szechenyi, all done up in her best frock and hat, her eyes flashing. He knew she rarely left Vienna and for a minute he was touched, but then he realised wild horses wouldn't have kept her from witnessing the event of the decade! Dear Yella, she had a ragbin of a mind, but she was very warm-hearted and so informative. Slowly over the next half hour, he effaced himself to check on the whereabouts of certain implements he would need soon – a fence cutter, a spade, an axe and one or two other items. He found them in the gardeners' workshop near the stables and put them into the back of a small car he planned to borrow.

At exactly 14.00, Mr Butler turned up with the two British lorries filled with provisions for the journey. There were also four burly men to unload it all into the train. Butler reported that their train had left Nord Bahn station as planned with its escort and the two cars on board. It was on route for Kopfstetten, the station only two miles distant from the castle. When Strutt got back to the castle, he found the Emperor standing in the great hall with great dignity and warmth, giving out gifts to all the staff.

At 14.30, some local schoolchildren saw the back of a huge train as it arrived at the station. Soldiers jumped out to fix Union Jacks at each end and on each side. Seven armed British police came out to stand guard. After a while, lorries and a horse-drawn wagon arrived full of baggage. There was a feeling of urgency.

At tea time, just before dark, Strutt told Ashmore he would be back soon and drove out of the grounds in the small car to the intersection of the Vienna-Pressburg-Marchegg telegraph wire which he had previously scouted out. He got out and with his torch as guide, found the tools in the boot. He then scrambled over the bracken at the side of the road up to a telegraph pole and proceeded to hack it down with the axe. He did the same to five other poles. He then dragged the severed wires about two hundred yards apart. If Renner and his men invaded the castle after their departure, he would find all the lines to Switzerland down. He would not be able to stop them from there. It was a filthy, muddy job in the dark and he swore profusely while he was doing it.

Two hours later, bathed and freshly dressed, he left his room in the schloss and approached the top of the stairs where the Emperor was supervising the descent of a two huge trunks which were full of household memorabilia and Habsburg private documents and records. Six men were heaving the trunks, while another man came along carrying a smaller, but very handsome brass-studded chest. The Emperor, whom he was glad to see was looking much better, grinned at him and whispered 'that chest contains the full story of the Mayerling tragedy in 1889. It was hushed up at the time, but I dare say you heard of it, yes?'

'I remember that the Foreign Office was fascinated by the whole story,' replied Strutt, 'but I never heard the details.'

This was a diplomatic white lie. The Foreign Office had long since ferreted out the whole story. On 30 January 1889, at Mayerling, the royal hunting lodge southwest of Vienna, Crown Prince Rudolph, the only son of Emperor Franz Joseph, shot dead his sixteen year old mistress, Baroness Mary Vetsera and then himself. The whole ghastly story was immediately hushed up. They put out the report that Prince Rudolph had died in a hunting accident and a full State funeral was conducted in the Cathedral. The Baroness was never mentioned and her family was bought off. Years later, when the story did get out piece by piece, it was first considered a murder/suicide, then a suicide pact, then a murder again by unknown agents. The incident was silenced for many decades.

'A sad story,' said the Emperor. 'His parents were badly affected.'

Zita then came up dressed for travel. She greeted Strutt and then asked him if he would keep safe some of her jewellery on the journey. She held out to him her fabulous pearls, six rows and the 'Maria Theresa' diamond stomacher, a huge brooch of diamonds in an atrocious design. He had no sooner pocketed these, when to his surprise, some of the other noble ladies came up asking for the same service.

Very soon, his pockets were so bulging with treasure, he was reduced to putting the overflow into his haversack. The Emperor then handed him a wallet full of money and Strutt had no other recourse, but to put that inside his jacket. 'I don't think I should share the Imperial car, do you, Sir?'

'Not tonight, Colonel. No.' Karl's eyes were clouded with unhappiness as he turned to his Empress and held out his arm for her. 'Are you ready, my darling?'

With all eyes upon them, Karl and Zita, the last Emperor and Empress of Austria-Hungary processed down the stairs arm in arm, Gussel at their side. Behind them walked little Archduke Otto, looking grave. The two countesses and Count Hunyady each carried a royal child and two nannies followed with the babes. All the servants and friends waiting below in the huge ornate hall fell to their knees on the marble floor. It was terribly sad. It was almost a relief to see the comical figure of old Maria Josefa, the Emperor's mother, hung like a Christmas tree with jewels, waddling down the steps with her two mangy collies on leads.

As she passed Strutt, at the bottom of the stairs, Countess Bellegarde whispered 'For heaven's sake, lose those dogs before we get on the train!'

It was completely dark outside. Only the automobile lights and a few lights falling from the schloss illuminated the courtyard which was full of silent people. Suddenly, there was the sound of shots in the distance. Strutt, already strung out with nerves, flinched then immediately raised his hands for everyone to keep silent. Ashmore, conferring with Shonta, told him there were poachers, or someone, out there again. Strutt motioned for everyone to make haste. The Imperial Family and their entourage got into the cars assembled on the drive and softly called their goodbyes to all the well-wishers huddled around them.

'Auf wiedersehen, Gott segne dich, lieber Kaiser,' rolled through the crowd like a sussuration through the trees. Once everyone was on board, a quiet command set the convoy of cars moving. One last truck followed behind with more baggage. Strutt and Ashmore shared the first car with Shonta. Two policemen from the British Food Commission sat in front with the driver. They were on red alert. The sounds of shooting faded away. So far, so good.

As the cars turned left into Kopfstetten, it started to drizzle, but not too badly. When they arrived at the station, Karl and Zita with the children were amazed to find the magnificent Imperial train waiting for them on the track, smoke pouring from the funnel. They were spellbound for a minute, they had never imagined this. There it sat in full array with the gilded engine gleaming in the light from their cars. There were three long saloon carriages, three sleeping cars, one kitchen, one dining car, two luggage vans and two extra open flat cars carrying the Imperial Rolls Royce and the big Daimler. Directly behind the engine flew a large Union Jack to suggest that the might of Britain was standing guard over everything.

Zita and Karl clutched each other's hand. The Colonel had kept his promise. They were not leaving like thieves in the night. They were leaving in proper style. Karl felt his eyes well with tears.

Strutt was horrified. The station was full of people. Where had they all come from? The car headlights and the light from the saloon cars lit up the nearest of some two hundred people. As far as he could judge, the road, fields and even the railway line were packed with villagers and peasants, some holding candles. All were silent; tears glistening in the flickering flames.

He and Ashmore got out of their car, thanked Shonta for his help, and walked briskly to flank the open door to the train. They stood at attention. The Imperial couple, followed them, waving to the crowd. The Emperor looked up and saw the Austrian soldiers from Eckartsau standing with rifles on top of the train. Once on board, Karl and Zita stood proudly waving from a window while everyone else boarded the train. They felt very emotional as they whispered their goodbyes.

When Strutt had seen everyone was safely onboard the train, he gave the signal to start and leapt aboard with Ashmore at his heels. As the wheels turned, a rumbling groan could be heard coming from the crowd. What a night to remember. The train gathered speed and slowly vanished into the dark, leaving behind only a pinpoint of light.

Chapter Twenty-Seven

March 23, 1919
On the Train

Inside the train, excluding the seven Austrian guards whom Strutt had thought prudent to take with them, there were twenty-five people, comprising the Imperial Family of seven, their private chaplain, Countess Bellegarde, Count Hunyady, Ledo, the two children's nannies, Strutt and Ashmore. The rest were servants, including the two admirable chauffeurs, Fritz and Heinz.

While the children were put to bed in their own compartment, Strutt walked the length of the train to make sure that everything was in order. He was pleased but not surprised to notice that all necessary for comfort had been built in, including a sink and lavatory in the luggage van, which was presumably designed to accommodate the Imperial dogs. At the farthest end of the luggage vans, he found Fritz having a smoke at the open window of the rear door. He was keeping an eye on the two cars nestled in the flat wagons beyond. Fritz saluted him. He was clean shaven, grave in demeanour and dressed in the grey Imperial livery, with two rows of gold buttons united by thin gold braiding criss-crossed between them. He had left his cap on the pile of baggage next to him. It didn't matter. These were extraordinary times. Strutt chatted with him briefly and then turned to retrace his steps.

The two luggage vans were piled high. He hoped everyone had packed a separate bag for the journey as it would be next to impossible to access anything from these vans. The cooks were working to prepare dinner, they had come on board earlier in the afternoon to get organised. Dinner would be served soon. Next came the dining car which the footmen were getting ready.

In the Imperial saloon, which was beautifully appointed with tufted sofas and chairs, he found Karl and Zita sitting alone enjoying a pre-dinner drink, Gussel at their feet. They immediately invited him to sit

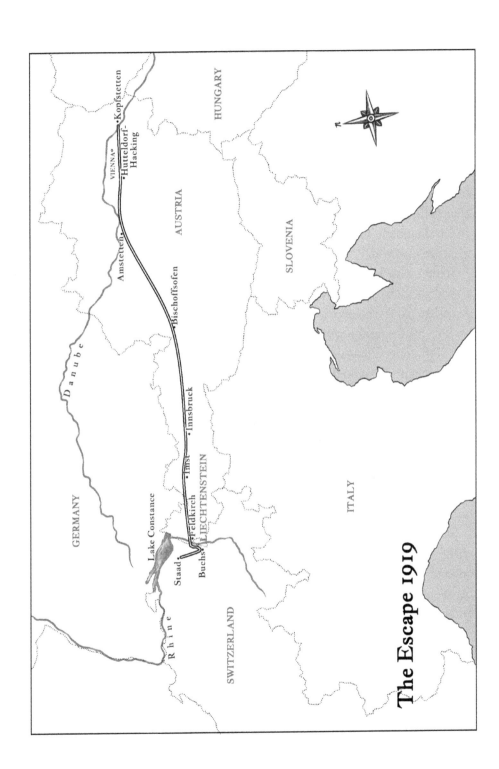

The Escape 1919

with them and Karl pushed a button to call a footman. Strutt sat and told them with relief that all was well for the present. He admitted he had had a bad moment when he saw the number of people who had come to see them off. The Emperor said he was also surprised, but also enormously gratified. Did Strutt think they may have difficulties because of it? Strutt hoped not, but they would soon know. He didn't trust Renner or his cohorts. At this point, the footman handed him a drink on a silver salver and Gussel got up from the Emperor's feet, padded over to Strutt and gracefully extend one paw.

Zita laughed. 'Gussel wants to shake your hand, Colonel. He knows what we owe you.'

Strutt, who had already shaken Gussel's paw several times since his arrival at Eckartsau, bowed and shook the extended limb with great sincerity. 'You've been of great help, Gussel. Thank you.' The dog padded back to his original position at the Emperor's feet and sank down with a sigh. Job done. They all laughed.

The Empress wanted to know what was going to happen next. Strutt told them the first stop that night would be after dinner at Hutteldorf-Hacking where the train would take on water. Until then, they could rest easy. He told them that for safety, he had ordered all window curtains to remain closed. He also suggested that now would be a good time for the Emperor to change into British uniform as planned.

'Quite right, Colonel. This is a British Food Commission train, is it not? We must all play our parts.'

Strutt's own compartment, at the end of the carriage, was crammed with his belongings and two of the Emperor's boxes. Ashmore was sitting on one of them standing guard, he looked fatigued. To cheer him up, Strutt teased him that one day he would be able to tell his grandchildren all about this adventure.

Ashmore was more interested in their safety. He didn't feel safe. Strutt agreed. It was a miracle they managed to get out of Kopfstetten. He had fully expected Renner to rat on his promise and send a regiment to stop them. Strutt shrugged out of his tunic. Of course, anything could happen, but first he was going to have a lie down. It was very possible that Renner had arranged for them to be stopped somewhere outside his own district. Then he could blame someone else if it went wrong. He wasn't going to worry about it for the moment. He untied his shoe laces and told

Ashmore to stop worrying and have a rest before dinner. It was going to be a long night.

Dinner for everyone in the dining car was subdued, and the Emperor and Empress joined them. They all knew they were at risk, but their faith in Colonel Strutt gave them courage. Everywhere he looked, someone was smiling and holding up a wine glass to salute him. Strutt felt very alone and heavy with responsibility. If this went belly up, it would be a catastrophe. Zita, seeing his grim look tried her best to cheer him.

'Colonel, surely the worst is over? We got away. I'm sure we will have plain sailing now. Have some of this delicious cheese.' She filled a plate for him and added some grapes and passed it over.

Strutt made a big effort. He wanted to reassure her, but he wasn't going to lie. Until they reached Switzerland, they were in peril.

At 22.00 when they arrived at Hutteldorf-Hacking to take on water, Strutt and Ashmore stared grim-faced from the window at the huge crowd of rough-looking people pressed up against the barriers. It was difficult to see how many there were as the only light came from the front of the train and the ill-lit station itself. Strutt decided on a reconnaissance and left the train for a smoke. Ashmore, trembling with fright, remained at the door of the train watching.

The crowd was sullen, but not yet menacing.

'What is this train?' someone asked in German.

'Britisher', someone muttered.

Murmurs of resentment were heard as the crowd studied the British flags adorning the train. Strutt looked up at the water tower wondering how he could hurry things along. The crowd was getting tenser by the minute. They needed to leave immediately.

Suddenly, he looked in horror down the platform to see Maria Josefa shambling towards him with her two disgusting dogs obviously in need of a pee. She was festooned with jewellery which was catching sparks in the light. Presumably she had thought it safer to wear it all rather than pack it.

Strutt quickly walked up to her as the crowd rumbled to a roar and growled in his most intimidating German 'Get back onto the train this instant. Schnell!' She looked around her in confusion and her eyes widened in terror. She hadn't noticed the crowd.

'Schnell!' he shouted and she scuttled back into the train like a rabbit down a hole. Strutt followed her and looked up just in time to see the water tower arm remove itself from the train. They could proceed, thank God.

Maria Josefa re-entered her carriage to a barrage of shocked complaints from her fellow passengers. She was tearfully repentant, but that didn't stop the dogs from peeing on the floor in front of them. Countess Bellegarde shivered in disgust. 'Those dogs should be put down!' Other arrangements had obviously been made for the very polite Gussel.

Strutt seethed in fury. That stupid woman! Now all Vienna would know they had left and where they were going. A risky gamble had just become the longest of long shots. There was nothing to be done now but to play the hand. He needed a drink.

By 23.00, everyone was bedded down and Strutt, after having walked the train again from front to back, finally settled himself on a camp stool set against the wall outside the Imperial bedroom compartments. He had a huge revolver in his lap. Ashmore brought him some coffee from his outpost in the forward gangway and suggested ways they could use the policemen if they were stopped. Strutt became irritated with his blathering and told him to go to bed.

In the small hours, some peasants watching from a wooden hut in a distant field, marvelled at the flag-bedecked train with its golden light and trailing smoke. It glided through the landscape like something from another age, a phantom from a long forgotten dream. It was very late. Strutt dozed with his hand over his revolver. The train began to slow.

When it stopped, they were at Amstetten. Strutt and Ashmore got out onto the island platform. It was full of unarmed Swiss soldiers escorting a food train on its way to Vienna. An officer rushed up to him and asked if his train was the Imperial one en route for Switzerland? Strutt looked puzzled. The officer said he had had a telegram from the last station saying the Imperial train was coming through. Strutt told the officer in a very authoritative manner that this was the British Food Commission train going to Berne. The officer saluted and hurried off. Strutt muttered to Ashmore. 'Thank you for that, Maria Josefa.' He didn't think the officer more than half believed him. Mercifully, after a few minutes, their train switched off onto the Selzthal line. Renner would know this, of course, if he managed to get their itinerary from the Station Master in Vienna.

At about 5.00 they arrived at Bischoffsofen. As soon as it was light, Strutt slipped back into his compartment feeling very old and tired. Luckily, there was no lack of hot water in the bathroom, which made up for everything. At about 7.00, going back to his post, he met the Empress in the corridor, looking fully rested and happy.

'What have you done with your cannon?' she joked, referring to the very large revolver he had kept in his lap all through the night. She only saw the hilt of his usual side arm, a Beretta semi-automatic, in his holster. He grinned. 'It has gone to bed, unlike me, Majesty. Did you have a good night?'

She and the Emperor had slept very well knowing he was on guard, she said. Then, looking closely at his tired eyes, she put her hand on his sleeve and asked 'But how are you?' For a moment, the sympathy in her eyes was so warm, he feared she might embrace him.

'I'm fine. Don't worry. I'll have a good sleep tonight. How are the children?' He put his hand over hers. He knew how she felt.

'Oh', she laughed. 'With all the rocking of the train, they fell asleep immediately and have only awakened. The nannies are dressing them now. I just looked in on them. Otto heard us laughing about your big gun and asks if he might see it, please.'

Strutt laughed. He had become very fond of the precocious boy. 'Tell him I am at his disposal after breakfast.'

At 7.30, the chaplain celebrated Mass in the saloon. They passed through Zell-am-See, the lake still frozen over, then up the steep grade to Schwas. All the blinds were up now and people gazed curiously at the splendid train. At Schwas, which they ran through at full speed at Strutt's orders, they saw French police lounging about the platforms, presumably sent by the Allies to keep order. The familiar broad Inn Valley came into view and they arrived at Innsbruck at 09.45. The platforms were covered with masses of scruffy-looking Italian soldiers. The Duke of Aosta, commanding the 3rd Italian Army, had courteously sent his ADC to enquire whether they required anything. They had obviously heard the report about the Imperial train as well. Strutt, resigned, thanked the pleasant looking fellow, who retired saluting. Strutt was somewhat relieved. Maria Josefa had done them huge damage, but the odds seemed to be shorting in their favour.

The train was only supposed to take on more water here, but there was a delay. Strutt didn't like it. The scruffy Italian soldiers, lounging about in various stages of undress uniform, began to be curious about the passengers. Some even playfully started to climb on each other's shoulders to look into the Imperial windows. Gussel, taking umbrage at these strange faces peering in, leapt to the windows and started barking.

Hearing this, Strutt immediately pulled down the window on the nearest door to see what was happening. The rabble of Italian soldiers was making a nuisance. Looking around, he then spotted a totally unconcerned Italian officer and shouted to him in fluent Italian to control his men. By this time, the Austrian policemen they had brought with them were standing on top of the train with their rifles pointing downwards. An ugly situation was looming up, but the Italians soon lost heart and desisted.

After the train got underway again, Strutt went to the dining car and awarded himself a very good breakfast. Count Hunyady joined him and thanked him for dealing with the Italians. 'The word is the Italians did not acquit themselves well in the war. Is it true?'

Strutt was on his second cup of coffee and feeling much restored. The truth was for the most part the Italian troops fought well, considering the lack of professional direction, administration and supply. Hunyady had to remember that before 1914, Italy was linked with Germany and Austria. The Triple Alliance they called it. Well, when war was declared, it turned out Italy was only interested in gaining back territory it felt belonged to it, namely, Trieste, Istria, Zara and Dalmatia. So she declared herself neutral, pending negotiations with each side. Whoever offered her the return of her lost territories at war's end, would win her support in the battles to come. Naturally, they expected the Central Powers to win the bid, but in the event it was the Allies who did so. All parties signed the London Pact in 1915. In return for the lost territory, Italy would fight with the Allies.

Unfortunately, the politicians neglected to take the military into their confidence on this. So, in 1915 after the London Pact was signed, the Military was vastly surprised to be told they were not to fight the Allies, but the Central Powers whom they had been planning to join!

'That doesn't explain why their reputation is so bad', said Hunyady frowning.

Strutt reached for a cigarette. Good troops will always fight badly when they are ill supplied and morale is allowed to deteriorate. Puffing out a smoke ring, he told Hunyady a story he probably wouldn't believe, but was probably true. It was said that the Italian Commando Supremo, General Cadorna was very fond of holding summary executions after lost battles. He believed in rule by terror not by inspiration. To him a battle was lost because his troops did not have enough courage to resist. Morale was everything to him, not guns or ammunition. Therefore, if the battle was lost, it was clearly the soldiers fault and he punished them.

Hunyady was shocked. It was no wonder then that their losses were so enormous. What a ghastly story. 'Everyone says how useless the Italians were, but maybe there was good reason.'

Strutt told him war was bloody, as Hunyady knew. In mitigation, the Italians did very well in 1918 at Vittorio Veneto when they had British troops fighting at their side. By that time Cadorna had been replaced.

Hunyady took awhile to process this enlightening information. Then he was curious about his own countrymen. What was their reputation? He had to brace himself for Strutt's reply. Hunyady knew perfectly well that most of the Hungarian nobles had stayed out of the war.[1] This was not good. On the other hand, most of the peasants had joined the Imperial regiments. He wasn't sure about them.

Strutt was surprised to be asked this question. Surely after Przemysi, Hunyady had no need to worry about the bravery of his countrymen? The Siege of Przemysi took place in Eastern Galicia in September 1914. The Russians, who outnumbered the Austro-Hungarians by over two to one, surrounded the fort for 133 days. The fort was finally forced to surrender, but not before destroying everything of value within its walls.

Hunyady knew this, of course, but he was upset that so many of his countrymen had died so bravely with nothing to show for it. A defeat was not going to aid them in the coming treaty negotiation either.

Strutt couldn't help looking at him with great commiseration. He was sorry. What could he say? Being on the losing side was a bad place to find oneself. Would Hunyady's estates be all right? Strutt knew they were outside Budapest somewhere.

---

1. This seems to have been a common opinion in some circles, but it has not been verified.

Hunyady shifted in his seat. He thought so, he hoped so. The Festhetics had just recently gone out to have a look. He was waiting to hear. Did Strutt know his lands marched with that of the Festhetics? Strutt vouchsafed he knew they were somehow neighbours.

All this was irrelevant really, Hunyady was much more concerned now for their Majesties. What was going to happen next? He thought Karl a good man, but weak. As a newly enthroned Emperor he had tried his best to stop the war, but he wasn't strong enough to influence real change and now his health was not good. In Hunyady's confidential opinion, Zita had twice his courage, but she was only a woman.

Strutt agreed. Leaning forward, he lowered his voice. 'Yes, and she's pregnant most of the time, I know, but Count, I have great faith in her. She is a lioness. You will see. They will come out of this all right somehow.'

The Count looked upset. Gabriella was worried, too. She and Agnes had worked like demons to help Zita hold everything together at Eckartsau. He had never been more impressed then when he had arrived and saw how it was.

Strutt agreed, he was impressed as well. He told Hunyady men discount the abilities of women too much. They treat them as inferiors, but they could probably run the world a lot better than men given the chance! Hunyady was amused at the idea.

Neither man was particularly cheered by their moment of confidentiality, but it was good to know they felt the same about some things. They went their separate ways.

Chapter Twenty-Eight

March 24, 1919
Wartegg

Later, Strutt walked back down the carriages to the Imperial sitting room. The Emperor was just finishing a late breakfast. He asked if he had slept well. Karl was in good spirits, he had slept better than he had expected and was feeling positively optimistic this morning. He looked up gaily at the Colonel and thanked him. 'It's all due to you, you know.'

Strutt reflected how much easier life would be if one didn't think so much. If one could rest one's problems on another's shoulders. He had never found shoulders broad enough himself. Despite all his optimism, the Emperor then sought reassurance that all would be well.

Strutt told him he thought so. They were almost at Switzerland. The next stop would be the last before the Swiss frontier. At Imst they would put on a mountain engine to take them through the Brenner Pass. If there was going to be trouble, this would be Renner's last opportunity. Strutt's gut told him Renner had missed his chance. It was going to be all right.

At Imst the train stopped to change engines. It was a tricky, but beautifully executed manoeuvre. The Empress, huddled in furs against the biting air joined Strutt on the platform to watch how it was done. Idly, she asked him what he would do when all this was over and he was home again.

He told her he supposed there would be a battalion somewhere waiting for him and, then he would come back and do more climbing in these mountains. She was fascinated to learn he was an experienced Alpine mountaineer and that he had written several articles on the subject. She asked him if his wife was a climber, too.

Strutt smiled. No, she wasn't a climber, but she was a great skier. Next winter, with luck, they hoped to be back at St. Moritz again like old times, except it wouldn't be like old times, would it?

Zita agreed with him as they watched the old engine being gracefully replaced by the new one from the siding by means of winches. Nothing would ever be the same again, but they must go on. What else could they do? She and his Majesty would not give up. They had responsibilities, children. She wished...

Here it comes, thought Strutt. She had been trying to ask him for something earlier. She made a lovely picture wrapped up in her furs, her big eyes looking at him appealingly. A bit flustered, she shyly put out her hand. 'Colonel, may I call on you for advice in the coming days? I know I have no right to ask after all you have done for us.'

Strutt listened with some sympathy. Yes, he was a British officer and owed them nothing. In fact, the situation was quite to the contrary, and yet...

'Somehow you always seem to know what to do.' Tears welled in her eyes. This was difficult for her. 'I might need you,' she whispered. Strutt took her hand tightly in his and told her ardently that she must know he was hers to command. No matter where he was, he would do everything in his power to help her. Surely she had realised that? Zita took her hand back and gave him a sweet enigmatic look he remembered all his life. She thanked him and lightly ran to the train steps. She must go and tell the Emperor, he would be so glad.

As they reboarded the train, they heard the sound of marching feet. Hurrying to the windows of the Imperial sitting room, they saw two dozen British soldiers form up at the end of the platform. Two of them were colour guards carrying the Austrian and British flags which were smartly streaming in the breeze. The Emperor seated at the window was astonished. It looked very much like a guard of honour.

'Look at that, my love! What is it?' As the train began to depart, the soldiers presented arms and saluted the Emperor. 'Oh', he said reaching for his handkerchief. 'Oh.'

The Empress was very moved and looking at Strutt. 'To think we have to thank our former enemy for this farewell from our own country...'

At this point, she could hear the Emperor sobbing for the first and only time and went to him. 'Thank you,' she said softly over her shoulder. Strutt, embarrassed for them all, quickly removed himself and shut the door.

Back in the saloon, Ledo was in tears, so immensely touched was he by the honour guard. Strutt was puzzled. He couldn't figure out from which unit the troops were composed. Who had ordered this? Not Cuninghame, surely?

The train crawled up the steep grade past Laneck-Pettneu, past the giddy Tisane viaduct, then Flirsch and stopped at St. Anton at the eastern entrance of the great Arlberg Tunnel. Strutt was chatting his way through the passenger carriages. Most of them had put their beds up and opened their doors. Gabriella was knitting a sweater while listening to one of the nannies read a story to Adelheid and Robert. Otto was standing at the window. He could see some men on horses. Did the Colonel know who they were?

Strutt went to look out of the window. In the distance he saw what looked to be cavalry riding in quite deep snow. He thought they must be Italians. They were near to Italy, he told the boy. If he was interested, he would tell him a story about the mountains. Smiling, Gabriella moved away from the window to give him room on the seat.

Strutt sat down and proceeded to tell Otto the names of the two big mountains in front of them – Roiffler and Parseierspitze. He knew their names, he said, because they were the first two mountains he ever climbed. Otto was fascinated to hear about his hero's first expedition and all it entailed. How old had he been then?

Strutt looked down at the bright intelligence of the little boy and felt something inside him move. He didn't often have dealings with children. In fact, thinking back, not much at all. His sister, Laura, had three daughters, but he hadn't seen them in years. So Otto was very special for all sorts of reasons. He liked the little fellow. He told him he was just seventeen in 1891 when his uncle allowed him to go up the mountains with friends from school. It had been great fun.

Otto told him he, too, would like to climb mountains when he was old enough. Would Strutt take him one day? His eyes were sparkling as he looked up at him. Strutt gravely assured him that if his father approved, he would certainly consider it.

Gabriella asked him if he had been at school nearby, Strutt looking appreciatively at the passing landscape, answered that he had been at Feldkirch School. Did she know it? Gabriella laughed. She certainly did.

Her brother had been there and even now, Prince Gaetano de Bourbon-Parma, the Empress' younger brother was studying there.

They then ran through eight miles of tunnel to Braz – the noise was deafening – and were no sooner out of the tunnel when they had to stop to let an eastbound train pass. It was the first train they had seen coming from the opposite direction. Strutt then told Otto that in 1892, his train had been buried for seven hours on this same spot when an avalanche had fallen across the line. They'd had to be dug out. Otto was agog. Were they safe now?

While they were chatting, the passengers on the eastern bound train were crowded at the windows staring at the fully recognisable Imperial train flying the British flag. The newspapers the next day said they had cheered the Emperor vigorously, but it wasn't true. After a time, Ledo came along and he and Strutt went to join the Imperial couple in their saloon and sat with them until they reached Feldkirch.

The Empress told him her younger brother was at school there. How she wished there was time to stop and see him. Strutt told her he also had been a student there at one time. At this point Ledo piped up to rather stridently ask him what they were going to do when the officials found they haven't got any passports? He was waving his hands and fussing about it. Strutt assured him there wouldn't be any trouble about it. Not to worry.

Zita wanted to know how he came to study at Feldkirch. Strutt told her he had shown a talent for languages as a boy and so once he had completed his studies at boarding school, his family had sent him to Felkirch to perfect his German. He had loved it there because it gave him a chance to ski and climb mountains, two things he still enjoyed doing.

Zita sighed and Karl's eye wandered to the window. The war was over for Colonel Strutt and he could go back to normal life. What would normal life now mean for her? Zita recovered herself after a moment or two and smiled at Strutt. He had earned a safe and happy future. She wished him well. Strutt, himself, felt conflicted with emotion. The train slowed and stopped. They had reached Feldkirch.

M. Weber-Deteindre, a Swiss gentleman in a top hat, frock coat and thick brown side whiskers, met Strutt on the platform and courteously introduced himself. He was there to inform them that the authorities were waiting to officially receive them into Switzerland at Buchs, the next station. They would then travel on one more station to Staad, where they would be greeted by the Duchess of Parma herself. Strutt asked him if transport had been organised there to take them all to Wartegg?

'The Duchess has seen to everything, Colonel, you will be pleased to know.'

'My thanks, sir,' he said as he bowed farewell. Privately, he wondered what Zita's mother, the Duchess of Parma, would be like. Was she as efficient as her daughter? They would soon find out.

The train started at once and he told everyone to be ready. Buchs was only an hour away. The Emperor's valet went to help him change into ordinary civilian garb. Strutt himself went to check all his boxes.

They soon ran across the Rhine and were in Switzerland. The journey had passed without an incident of any kind, if one excluded Maria Josefa's near criminal walk down the platform at Hutteldorf-Hacking. Strutt was elated.

The chief waiter in the dining room chose this moment to come up and present him with a bill for the journey. Strutt was astonished. That Renner had the gall to do this, just beat everything! He was standing there seething when Ledo joined him fussing about something else and seeing him upset, rather fearfully asked what was the matter now. Strutt showed him the bill. It was for 8000 krona. Ledo paled, but loyally said that, of course, the Emperor would pay. Strutt, furious at being in this embarrassing position, insisted he would sign on behalf of the British government, but Ledo insisted on paying in cash and so it was.

At Buchs station, Swiss troops, wearing new lovat green uniforms and steel helmets, were lined up at attention on both sides of the track. Their journey had almost ended. On the platform waiting for them was Monsieur FH Borsinger de Baden of the Swiss Foreign Office, Colonel Bridler, commanding the 6th Infantry Division and several of his staff. A large and respectful crowd were kept well in the background by more troops.

They greeted Strutt with the utmost courtesy and cordiality and after a few minutes conversation; Strutt led them onto the train and presented them to the Their Majesties. He then left them with the Imperial Couple and went off to send two hurried telegrams.

On returning, he found the seven Austrian police officers who had accompanied them standing at attention by the train, along with

Ashmore, all grinning broadly. Ledo was presenting each man, on his Majesty's behalf, with a silver watch with the Imperial monogram and a cigarette case embossed with the Austro-Hungarian and Habsburg arms. They were very pleased and Ashmore was delighted. The police officers were to wait at Buchs while the train took the rest of the party on to Staad. It would then return to take them back to Vienna.

M. de Baden, Colonel Bridler and his staff joined them on the train for the thirty minute journey to the tiny station of Staad. There, once again they found a guard of honour waiting, but this time the Duchess of Parma, with several members of her family, including the Duke of Braganza were with them on the platform. They had made it. Zita was home.

Strutt melted away to make sure the Swiss military and railway authorities were properly organised to deal with the vast quantities of luggage. They were as usual immensely efficient. Shortly, Colonel Bridler, a very capable-looking type, conveyed Strutt and Ashmore in his car to an hotel in Rorschach and overpowered him with kindness and what seemed like a hundred food vouchers. The Colonel was very sorry that they could not put him up at the Castle, but he would understand that space there was very limited now that so many people had arrived.

He looked at Strutt with a frank smile. As another soldier, he felt confident that Strutt would prefer to be comfortably separate. Strutt gave him a relieved smile and shook his hand. He couldn't have been more right.

'Now', said Bridler, 'you are free to go everywhere and anywhere and do as you like, but there is one condition.' Strutt couldn't think what it could possibly be.

Bridler laughed at his bewilderment. 'You may not wear your sword!'

'My sword?!' cried Strutt surprised. 'I haven't seen that article since I was wounded in 1914. Fear not that I will frighten the populace with it.' He bowed.

Bridler left smiling and Strutt went to unpack. He was still tense. He went downstairs to Reception to fire off some more telegrams. The first was to Sir Victor Rumbold at the War Office asking him to telegraph him 1000 Swiss Francs, as he was running low on money. Rumbold obligingly replied within the hour. He then telephoned out to Wartegg, only two miles away, to tell Countess Bellegarde that he would come to them the following morning unless he was elsewhere required. She said that was perfectly all right. The family had a lot to talk about that night.

Then he astounded the hotel manager with a request to leave 'a few valuables' in the hotel safe overnight. They needed three steel boxes to hold all the jewellery he was carrying. He had already given Ledo back the wallet full of money at the station.

Finally, having completed all his chores, Strutt went back up to his room and told Ashmore to see to the laundry and polish everything else up. Then he had a good look around the room. The job was finished and he could relax. He took off his shoes and tunic jacket and lay down on the bed. By God, it was a miracle they had got through. Surely this would be the end of it now? His eyes closed.

Chapter Twenty-Nine

March 25, 1919

I n the morning, after the best sleep he had had in three months, Strutt woke up thinking of Zita. What would happen now? Could Karl regain the throne of Hungary? Recent reports said that a revolution was going on there. Bela Kun, a communist, had just seized power in Budapest and proclaimed Hungary a Soviet Republic. It didn't look good. Technically, Karl was still the King, but he would need the support of the Allied powers to regain the throne. Strutt pondered this while he took breakfast in his room.

At 9.30, he received a message saying that Count Ledohoffski was awaiting him downstairs to take him to Wartegg Castle. He finished dressing and went down to the Daimler. Ledo looked rested and relaxed. His gentle nature had shed itself of all the recent horrors and endless difficulties and regained its normal happy balance. Here was a jovial Ledo come to greet him.

After the usual small talk, they set off for Wartegg, which was only two miles away. Ledo immediately told him how lucky he was to be staying at the hotel. He would not believe how crowded the Castle was. He, himself, was having to share a room and was lucky to have the bed. Fortunately, there was talk that some people might be leaving soon, so they would be a bit more comfortable.

Strutt asked him how the Imperial Couple were faring this morning? Ledo beamed. How could they be anything less than ecstatic to be out of Austria and with the Empress' mother again? They had always been close.

They were driving through mountains and came out to a view of Lake Constance. There before them was Wartegg Castle sitting on the shore surrounded by a small wood of sparse trees. Strutt didn't think the chateau had much appeal. It looked like an ordinary medium-sized, old fashioned chateau, but perhaps the interiors belied the exterior. The drive wound through a pretty garden and then they were there.

To Strutt's dismay, the whole party was outside on the drive waiting to greet him with cheers, applause and pats on the back. He did not enjoy the experience. To his further discomfort, when he was presented to the Duchess of Parma, he feared for a horrid moment she was going to kiss him! He did not smile and sensing his discomfort, she backed off, but with a twinkle in her eye.

It didn't take long for Strutt to appreciate this mother of his Empress. Over the next few days, he got to know her quite well. She was only in her late forties, still young-looking with pretty dark hair and a pleasant face given to laughter. Strutt found her extremely gracious and sympathetic. A daughter of the deposed King Miguel of Portugal, she had married Robert, Duke of Parma, as his second wife in 1884 and had produced no less than twelve children to match the twelve he had already from his first wife. The Bourbon-Parmas were terrific breeders. Unfortunately, when the consanguinity between the parents was too close, as was the case with the first wife, Princess Maria Pia of the Two Sicilies, the children produced were sometimes mentally retarded. Five of these step-children were being looked after in the Castle at the moment.

At dinner the first night, they dined in what could only have been the ball room, it was so large. As usual, the walls and ceilings were gilded, frescoed and carved, but this time there were more candles in evidence. It was a gay family party. He was seated on the Duchess' right so that she could do him honour and express her eternal gratitude more fulsomely. This embarrassed Strutt, so he cut in to tell her he had had the honour of meeting both of her sisters -- the Archduchess Marie Thersien at Biarritz in the summer of 1912 and Duchess Karl Thodor of Bavaria at a shooting lodge outside of Munich a year later. 'I'm sure you know there is a great family resemblance between the three of you. Your sisters are both charming women.' He sat back in his chair with a glass of wine in his hand and smiled at her. The Duchess laughed. He was diverting her from talking about him.

'Colonel, I fear you know quite a lot about me. I shall have to write to my sisters immediately to find out all about you!' It was easy to see where Zita had got her looks and charm, Strutt thought, but Zita's intelligence was all her own.

The Duchess asked him if he had, by chance, ever met her husband who had died some years before. Strutt was genuinely sorry to have to reply in the negative. He would have liked to have met a man with such a prodigious progeny. All he seemed to know about him was that he spoke many languages and was very cosmopolitan.

It was true, she said. The Bourbon-Parmas spent time in Italy, France and Austria and could lay claim to citizenship in all. Her husband considered himself a Frenchman, although his main house was in Austria. Consequently, the children felt at home in all those countries. How could they not? This could be confusing for people who were not well travelled themselves.

Down the table, chatting a mile a minute, Strutt could see Zita at her most sparkling. She was delighted to be home with her mother and to be safe again. There was so much to catch up on.

The party now staying at the chateau was uncomfortable. It was not a very large house to begin with and there were fortunately two or three small chalets in the grounds as well, but it was not enough. Strutt figured that besides the train party of twenty-five, there was the Duchess and five of her step-children. (Strutt called these adults 'soft' in his diary). Then there was the Duchess' own family of seven, her brother the Duke of Braganza and his wife and their very pretty daughter, the Infanta Elizabeth. Next came four ladies-in-waiting, two priests and a sort of General ADC – a rather grim fellow called von Werckmann who had been an officer in the Emperor's former Hussar Regiment. It was a mystery to him how they all managed to stow themselves away. The servants must be stacked up in the basement. How lucky he was to be quartered in the hotel at Rorschach.

The Duchess begged that he share his meals with them at Wartegg. 'You cannot mean to leave us all alone without your company?' she said. Strutt smiled his acceptance. There were at least thirty people at lunch and the same at dinner. A certain amount of ceremony was kept up as the Emperor and Empress were present, but it was all quite familiar.

That first night, after dinner, Strutt had a long talk with the Duke of Braganza, Zita's uncle. The Duke had commanded an Austrian Cavalry Corps in 1918 and had been captured by the British with all his staff on the Piave River in the final battle of Vittorio-Veneto. As Strutt well knew, this battle was fought in freezing conditions on the Austria/Italian Front during October and November the year before. The antagonists were a consortium of Italian, British, French and American forces against

Austria-Hungary. The ensuing defeat of Austria and the Central Powers finished the war on that Front.

Braganza bore no grudges. He was a cultured and well-travelled man. He could not give sufficient praise to the British and the way he and his men had been treated as a prisoners-of-war. He also shared the general contempt of most of the Allies for the Italians. Did Strutt know that of the six hundred thousand Austrian prisoners claimed by the Italians, nine-tenths had been captured *after* the Armistice? He was appalled. Strutt told him he had already heard this from several British sources. Braganza knew the British well, having travelled and shot much in India when he was younger. He had a certain arrogant charm which appealed to Strutt. They would talk again.

Finally, Strutt excused himself and sought out Ledo. The two of them agreed they would proceed to Berne early the next day by train. Before leaving for his hotel, he threaded his way through the group of family surrounding her sofa to delight the Empress with the jewellery she had entrusted to him wrapped up in a bright blue box provided by the concierge. Everything had been delivered to Switzerland safe and sound.

Chapter Thirty

April 1, 1919

The end of March quickly moved into April. There was heavy and continuous snow, brightened occasionally by blinding sunshine. On a gentle slope in the castle gardens, Otto and Adelheid often played on their toboggan, never tiring of going up and down. Zita, Gabriella and Hunyady kept an eye on them while they circled the paths.

One morning, Strutt was out walking with them feeling utterly relaxed, when his boot was hit by a snow ball. Looking down he saw little Robert in great glee, waiting to see what he would do. For a moment he was non-plussed, but then pretending to be wounded he let out a cry 'Ladies, we are under attack!' He then picked up a very small snow ball and threw it gently at Robert. 'Take that you little villain!' All the ladies laughed. In a minute Otto and Adelheid had joined the fight which expanded when Zita had a go at them as well. At this point there was a great shout from the terrace above them.

'Courage, Otto, Papa is coming', the Emperor came rushing down the steps, grabbing a bit of snow as he ran and threw it straight at Strutt's chest. Boom. Strutt was a bit shocked, but nevertheless played his role to the hilt.

'I've been hit! This is the end,' he yelled as he fell to one knee, his head lowered to one arm. The children all stopped, appalled at what they had done. Robert looked like he was going to cry.

'Don't be fooled, *leiblinge*,' said Zita laughing. 'He is just pretending to be hurt. Watch!' And she threw a snowball at his shoulder. Taking his cue, Strutt raised his head and grinned at Robert who threw himself down on him squealing. Otto and Adelheid rushed to help him up.

After that to his surprise and gratification, he became very good friends with the children. Otto would often seek him out with his book of maps. The boy was eager to have their journey traced for him and to know where Strutt's battles had taken place. He was a very serious boy and protective of his father, whom he knew to be frail. On the other hand, he also loved to run and jump with Adelheid. Twice Robert brought Strutt a book for him to read. The little boy would hand him the book, climb into his lap and put his thumb into his mouth. Strutt would then read from Tales of Jemima Puddle Duck or Benjamin Rabbit in English. One wet afternoon, Adelheid joined them and leaned on his arm for a reading of Cinderella. It was an education, Strutt had never considered children to be amusing and so he relished his time with these three. He asked Zita why she read Beatrix Potter to the children when there were so many German fairy tales to be had.

Zita smiled with a twinkle in her eye. Had he ever read any of them? No, he hadn't. He seemed to remember in those days trains were all that interested him, as he had a vast train set as a boy.

Then he wouldn't know how brutal most of the German fairy stories are. They were not written for children, she told him, but for adults and the times were cruel. Very few of the stories had happy endings.

So that was why she preferred Beatrix Potter. Of course, there was another more practical reason. Reading to them in English helped them to learn the language. Strutt was much struck by this.

He asked her how many languages she spoke. She replied, six – French, German, Portuguese, English, Italian and Spanish. They all did. When she was a child they always seemed to be moving. Her father had houses in France, Austria and Italy and they spent a lot of time with her mother's family as well in Portugal and Spain. Her parents had a rule, they must always speak the language of the country in which they were in. That way it was quite easy to learn. They were taught English by tutors. She used to complain about that as it was rare to meet an Englishman then. She was glad now.

Through the days, visitors came and went. On 3 April, the Emperor sent a telegram to King George requesting that Strutt be allowed to remain with him. Strutt knew nothing of this 'officially', but it was he who put it into good English to be telegraphed to the British authority at Berne. Fortunately, he had already moved to circumvent this request by writing on March 25th to the War Office, asking that he should be returned forthwith either to London or to Constantinople, where he was supposed to be going before this adventure intervened. He had done his job here and it would not be good to prolong his stay with Zita. Their friendship was strong now. If given more time, it might cause comment.

On 5 April, Charles Paravicini, the Head of the Political Department at Berne asked to see him. Strutt left Wartegg at 05.30 and got to Berne at 14.40 where he checked into the Bellevue Hotel. Later at the British Legation, Paravicini, an elegant gentleman with silver hair, told him the latest news.

First, the Emperor's brother, Archduke Max Eugen was to be allowed to come into Switzerland, but permission was definitely refused for Kary Czernin. The former Foreign Secretary of Austria still carried the taint of trouble and they didn't want him. Strutt was sorry to hear this. Poor Maritschy was going to be desolate at the news. She was desperate to leave Vienna. Karl had admittedly behaved badly, but Strutt knew that in confused times, many did. Unfortunately, Kary's mistakes of judgment was entirely too visible. He hoped he would be all right.

Second, Paravicini told him Taszilo Festetics had been murdered in his own home and that his brother George had been 'left for dead' on their return from Hungary on March 23rd. Strutt was appalled and upset. He later discovered to his relief that it wasn't true, but they had both been robbed of most of what they had been able to save from the wreck of their estates and both had been maltreated. This was terrible, but at least they were alive.

Later at the Legation Chancery, one the staff, Goodhart, handed him two telegrams which had arrived the night before.

From the War Office April 4th. *You will proceed forthwith to Constantinople.*

From the War Office to GCHQ Constantinople April 4th and forwarded to Berne: *Why has Strutt not returned to England?*

What monumental inefficiency, thought Strutt. He himself had sent a message on 25th March asking to return and these messages had not arrived until yesterday. That was eleven days in transmission. Clearly, there was no immediately reason for him to hurry. He knew the trains were still down between Bucharest and Constantinople and going there now seemed superfluous, so he wired Florrie to meet him in Paris on April 11th. He also telegraphed Wartegg to tell them his departure plans and that his return to them would be delayed until the 8th. There were some interesting people here in Berne he wanted to meet. He rarely missed a chance to gather intelligence.

At the end of dinner at a decent restaurant to which Goodhart was gracious enough to invite him, Commandant Herce, the Spanish Military Attaché, came up and asked to present Strutt to someone whose name he couldn't catch. Curious, Strutt rose and thanked Goodhart for an enjoyable dinner and said he would see him again in the morning.

The person who wanted to see him turned out to be Prince Alfonso of Spain,[1] husband of the pretty Beatrice of Coburg, who was a sister of Queen Marie of Romania. He was an excellent fellow and they had a long talk. Strutt met many other people that evening.

One of them was the once very attractive Princess of Pless[2] who subsequently wrote him a long and silly letter asking him to procure for her a British passport with which she could return to England. He ignored it. Surely she must have known the correct route for a British passport was through the Legation? Then he remembered, with a wry smile that she must have a dossier a mile high there, given all she had got up to during the last few years. Poor Daisy.

The next morning, he awoke with a hangover, which Ashmore fixed with his 'infallible cure.' He lunched with Paravicini and several other Swiss, including Borsinger, the First Secretary at the Embassy. Strutt was surprised by their gentlemanly manner and decided he must change his opinion of the Swiss. He thoroughly enjoyed himself. Later, he confided to his diary 'there are, after all some gentlemen in Switzerland!'

In the afternoon, he had tea with the Swiss President at the Houses of Parliament and ended the night by dining again with Goodhart and some of his colleagues. This turned out to be very amusing indeed as they knew all the gossip about everyone he had been meeting. He said his goodbyes to them with real friendship.

---

1. This was, in fact, Prince Alphonso, Duke of Galliera, born 1886. He was first cousin of King Alfonso XIII of Spain.
2. Born Mary Cornwallis-West, Daisy was a noted society beauty of the Edwardian period. She married Henrich XV, Prince of Pless, member of one of the wealthiest European noble families. Her extravagant lifestyle coupled with disastrous events and political family scandals, made her well known to the international press.

Over the years, Strutt had made it his business to cultivate knowledgeable people along the way, socially and militarily. This was one of the ways he kept informed of what was going on behind the scenes. In his view, to do a proper job, one needed to thoroughly understand what was behind some of the decisions he was given to execute. Blind obedience was an imperative for the troops, but a proper officer, in his opinion, needed to understand what he was about. When he was moved to Military Intelligence in 1915, this practice proved invaluable. Florrie always accused him of being an inveterate gossip, but it wasn't true. He was much more of a listener.

At the crack of dawn on 8th April, he boarded the 05.00 train back to Wartegg. It was time for him to leave them and he felt real sadness. He had truly come to have a great fondness for them all. Gabriella and Ledo with his stumbling sweetness, Hunyady with his stalwart charm. Most of all he would miss Zita and her happy moppets. The Emperor was something else. His lack of strength and naivety did not bode well and his poor health did not inspire confidence, but in spite of all this, one couldn't help liking him. This was perhaps odd, but true nevertheless. Zita would have to be strong for both of them.

At Romanshorn station, he found Ledo waiting for him with the Daimler. All was well, but Ledo told him with sadness in his eyes that there was great consternation at his approaching departure. Everyone in the castle had hoped he would be allowed to stay on with them. Count Hunyady met him at the front entrance on his return and offered him tea in a sitting room. He wanted a few words.

Count Joseph Hunyady had been with the Emperor ever since they were Captains of Hussars together in 1914. The old Emperor had asked him to keep an eye on the younger man, whose boyish gaiety had given some concern. No one had considered that Karl need worry about becoming the heir apparent for decades to come, which left plenty of time for him to fully mature. His uncle Franz Ferdinand was after all only fifty when he was killed.

Hunyady was genuinely sorry to see Strutt go. They would be forever in his debt. Strutt, too, was sorry as he would like to have stayed long enough to see the Imperial Couple permanently settled. What were Hunyady's thoughts on the matter?

The younger man, sat back in his chair. It would be difficult. He didn't think they would be able to stay at Wartegg long. It was just too crowded. Arrangements would have to be made for the extended family to find other homes. He and Gabriella would stay as long as they could.

Strutt asked him for news of his estates near Budapest. He'd been shocked by the attack on the Festhetics. Taszilo had been an old and dear friend.

Hunyady became agitated. He was suffering considerable strain under his urbane facade. In a low voice, he admitted he had been shocked as well. He knew he should go down to Keszthely himself, but he didn't feel he could leave their Majesties. His steward had sent him a message saying there had only been a few minor problems so far, so they might be all right. He hoped so. After they were married he and Gabriella planned to make their home at Keszthely. He prayed it would be possible, otherwise, they would have to make other plans.

Strutt studied his boots. It was hard to know what to suggest. Until they had a clear picture of their position, there wasn't much to say. There was the throne of Hungary, of course. The Emperor might make a play to get it back, what did Hunyady think about that? He was Hungarian.

Hunyady grimaced. His country was being over-run by Communists. A bandit called Bela Kun had taken control of the government. The monarchy was in abeyance. He thought it would take a very strong man to turn things around. He didn't see it happening, but he knew the Empress was determined to try. He had a devil of a time trying to persuade her to wait at least until the baby was born when things might be more settled.

Strutt was hit again by the helpless feeling that everything hinged on this small, vulnerable woman who perhaps had too much courage for her own good. At least they were safe for the present. The baby was due next month and her mother would look after her. Things might change by then. He bid Hunyady adieu and went up to change for dinner.

While he was dressing in his room, there was a small knock on the door and without waiting, his room was invaded by the Imperial children. Otto, Adelheid and little Robert crowded into his room crying '*Verlasse uns nicht, lieber Oberst!*' (Don't leave us, dear Colonel.) Strutt was hugely touched and didn't know what to say. The truth was always best, so he shook Otto by the hand and told him, man to man, that he was being called away to command a battalion.

Otto, being a bright boy, queried how this could be? The Colonel had told him there were no more wars! Regrouping, Strutt told him that was true for now, but there would always be another war some day and they must be prepared for it. That's what professional soldiers did.

He looked at the serious little face in front of him and at adorable Adelheid in her white cotton dress with the pretty lace at the bodice. Robert was clutching his knee possessively with a slight drool falling from his mouth. Strutt was unprepared to say more, so he stoked their heads and told them to run along. He promised not to leave without saying goodbye.

Otto took Robert's hand and Strutt watched them leave. There was tug at his heart. He and Florrie had missed out on something important, he realised now. Theoretically, they might just manage it now, but he felt far too old. He prayed all would go well for these children in the new world before them. It wasn't going to be easy.

Chapter Thirty-One

April 8, 1919
Farewell

After dinner, in a quiet room, he had a long talk with Their Majesties on the subject of what they should do next. Who might help them regain the Austrian crown; should they try for the throne of Hungary and if so, when. Karl was sure of the loyalty of Admiral Horthy who was dealing with the current communist revolution there, but would the Hungarians themselves welcome back the Monarchy? Karl and Zita thought they would. Failing all that, where could they go?

The coal in the fire was smouldering by the time they came to a conclusion. If all else failed, they would hope to settle in England, Strutt said he would do his best to make that happen and bade them goodnight. Tomorrow would be his last full day in Switzerland and there was a lot still to do.

He'd planned to rise early to take the 05.00 train again to Berne, but Prince Rene, one of Zita's brothers, said he would drive him there in his big Renault. It would be much quicker and much more pleasant. So in the morning, before leaving, much to his dismay, he was photographed, first by a reporter from '*L'Illusion*' magazine and then by nearly everyone else in the house. He avenged himself by taking the whole party with the Empress's camera, which sadly didn't turn out well.

In the early evening, when he was back from Berne, the children came to see him and shyly presented him with their photos. Archduke Otto laboriously wrote his signature on his and requested Strutt to go to Hungary now to make it much more '*kaiseur-tru*' for his Papa.

After dinner, he said goodbye to the Duchess and the Parma family and to his twenty-five train companions. He was quite overwhelmed by the praise heaped on his head for the little he had succeeded in doing. It was a relief when it was over. He then went to see Zita alone in her sitting room.

This was hard. There she sat on the soft, padded sofa by the bright fire, a tiny figure rounded with the next child to be born to her. She looked young and vulnerable, but he knew she was not. It seemed to him she had more strength of character in her little finger than in most men he knew. The bare fact that they had got to Wartegg was down to her foresight and planning. He had just provided the food and transportation.

She invited him to sit in the chair opposite. He watched her brilliant eye in the firelight as he told her how proud he was he had been able to be of service to them. Her guard was down. There was a short smile and humour lurked around the edges of it. 'I can't think you were pleased to be given the job in the first place, Colonel. Were you?' She laughed at the enigmatic look on his face. He wasn't going to lie to her and couldn't tell her the truth either. He told her he had no regrets, quite the contrary.

'You know we couldn't have done it without you, Colonel. You grasped immediately what the situation was and found solutions. The Emperor, for all his wonderful qualities, was not able to do that.'

Strutt replied gruffly while staring into the fire. 'His Majesty is very fortunate to have a woman like you as his Empress, ma'am. Women like you are one in a million.' He turned to look at her with admiration and affection. 'You are an eagle, Majesty, a veritable lioness....'

She interrupted him with a laugh. 'What nonsense. I don't think I can be compared to a lioness, Colonel, perhaps a small eagle. It got us here, as you say, but what happens now, I know not.' She paused, folding her skirt with her small hand and softly asked him 'Will you help us again, if we need it?' The look she gave him then was unlike anything he had ever before experienced. It was a call of like to like, of kindred spirit to its mate. He knew he would die for her if she asked it. How strange it was, but how totally unmistakeable.

'Send for me and I will come.' His look was a promise.

They talked for some little time. Finally, she stood and held out her hand. If they were different people and had met at a different time, who knows what might have happened? 'Goodnight, Colonel, until tomorrow.' Strutt knelt and kissed her hand. Before he left, she gave him a large framed photo of herself which always afterward held a place of honour in his study.

He then went to see the Emperor who was in excellent spirits. 'I won't say goodbye now, Colonel. The Empress and I are coming with you as far as Baden where we will have lunch. You know we cannot thank you enough for your great service to us, but more on that score tomorrow.' Strutt expressed his thanks and said it wasn't necessary. Karl smiled. 'We do not agree. Goodnight, dear Colonel.' Strutt bowed and took his leave. It was kind of them to travel so far, but his heart sank. He did not enjoy prolonged farewells.

At last, the final morning arrived. It was very cold, but sunny. Spring would not be long in arriving now. Indeed, the snow was melting and green shoots were sprouting everywhere. His kit along with Ashmore's was packed into the Renault driven by Prince Rene with Ledo in attendance. It was to follow the Imperial Rolls Royce carrying the Imperial Couple, Strutt and two drivers. They started off at 10.30. In the bright spring sunshine, the whole house party assembled on the drive to see them off. Strutt said goodbye to the children, who had drawn him a picture of the Rolls with Strutt as sole occupant. He was very touched by this. He would always remember their sweet faces.

The drive to Baden was quite outstandingly beautiful in the sunshine. Conversation was casual. They drove through the quaint town to the best hotel where a private room had been engaged for the whole party to lunch. (Ashmore dined in the tap room with the chauffeurs.) This was the end.

Strutt found he had little to say that had not been said already. The Empress and her brother, Prince Rene, kept up a light chat which got them through. Ledo even thought of one or two old jokes, but Strutt's thoughts were a world away on the strangeness of fate.

He had been brought across Europe to save this particular couple and their family who in normal circumstances, he would never have met; had no interest in meeting. He had successfully done so, but in the longer term was it the right thing to have done for them? He was very ambivalent about this. Could he have done better? By removing them, he may have ended their public lives forever. He hoped not. He wrote in his diary 'Had the noblest and bravest woman that ever graced a throne; the most loveable of men, the very soul of strictest honour...no further, higher, Destiny?' What if instead he had helped them to stand and fight? The Foreign Office would have loved that. No, there was no other choice. He had done the right thing. He just couldn't shake off an unease about their future.

At dessert, the Emperor presented Strutt with a solid gold cigarette case with his initials in diamonds on it. Afterwards, they walked up the road a bit. A few passersby stared curiously, but very respectfully at them and many saluted. Finally, they said goodbye. Her Majesty's last words to him were 'Only an Englishman could have accomplished what you have done for us; you are the rulers of the world.'

He once again knelt down to her and kissed her hand. People began to collect as the Emperor's car drove up. He last saw them waving their hands to him as the Rolls turned the corner back to Wartegg. At the last sighting, the Renault came up to him with Ashmore and the driver in front.

Strutt got into the back of the car. He felt like a bubble had burst. Could it really be all over? The last three months had been so extraordinary, so entirely bizarre; surely it had all been a dream? He laughed out loud, who would believe it?

Ashmore wanted to know what was so funny? Everything, he told him. Sometimes you just have to laugh at life in general. He felt like a new man. Asmore was sceptical. As far as he was concerned, the whole trip had been a nightmare and he couldn't wait to get home.

After driving on to Berne and thence to Geneva, Strutt and Ashmore got onto a chaotic French train which was unbelievably overcrowded and set off for Paris, where they arrived on April 12 and 07.00, one and a half hours late. He left Ashmore at the Gare de Lyon after profusely thanking him for his first class assistance and enjoined him to make haste to the British Embassy to find out where his Regiment had got to. Lastly, he gave him a letter addressed to his commanding officer giving a glowing report of Ashmore's part in an unmentioned secret endeavour for the Foreign Office. Ashmore glowed with pride and departed.

He then threw his bags into a taxi and drove to the Meurice to look for Florrie. By this time it was after 09.00. She might have gone down to breakfast. He quietly let himself into the suite to the sound of her talking on the telephone. Of course she was on the telephone. When was she not in bed of a morning chatting to her myriad girlfriends? They all did it. He smiled and walked softly to the bedroom door. There she was, her long brown hair over one shoulder, the telephone over the other. At the sight of him, she mumbled something to her listener, slammed down the receiver and leapt from the bed.

'Bill!' she cried, throwing herself into his arms for a big hug and a long kiss.

At this time, Florrie Strutt was thirty-six years old and still attractive with short brown hair that fell back in waves. Of middling height, she was very trim, her eyes were an engaging hazel under dark brows and she smiled often. She lived for skiing and walking and for the lively social round that accompanied both sports especially at St. Moritz. She and Strutt been a good team for fifteen years and she expected they would be an even better one now. The war, in spite of the long separations, had brought them closer. She had made it her business to study the Eastern Front carefully and his frequent letters had given her a fairly precise understanding of what he had been up against.

She pushed him back and looked him over carefully. He seemed calm and happy. How was that? She had expected a thoroughly weary and even haunted man to return to her. She had seen how quiet so many returned soldiers were. This husband of hers felt relaxed and somehow renewed. His last project must have been a success.

After five days resting up and talking constantly, Strutt received a message from the War Office instructing him to proceed to Constantinople to make his final report to General Tom Bridges as previously scheduled. They were both annoyed by this as what could it matter now? Nevertheless, it had to be done. This time Florrie went with him. She was not going to say goodbye to him again no matter what.

Two weeks later, after a rough crossing to Malta from Marseilles and an even rougher crossing in full gale to Constantinople, they arrived and were put up at Enver Pasha's[1] house. Florrie never wanted to see a ship again, but she soon picked up when they found General Francet d'Esperey, Strutt's old Supreme Commander and friend, also in residence. To his enormous surprise, the next day, his old friend awarded him his fourth

---

1. Enver Pasha 1881-1922 was a famous Turkish nationalist and rival to Mustafa Kemal, later Ataturk. He was one of the leaders in the 1908 Young Turk Revolution against Sultan Abdul Hamid II and one of the architects of the Ottoman-German Alliance in 1914. He rose to the rank of Pasha (Major-General), but proved ineffective in that role and had to be 'advised' by German military officers during the rest of the First World War. After the Armistice of Mudros was signed 30 October 1918, when the Ottoman Empire collapsed, he fled the country.

Croix de Guerre. Florrie was thrilled to be there to see it. Her chest filled with pride and her smile was like the sun.

It turned out this last award had nothing to do with his recent mission. In fact, no British official, no Parliamentarian, no Peace Treaty diplomats or Military personnel displayed the faintest interest in his late mission. Not even Florrie was particularly interested in anything but the bare bones of the thing, but he knew it would be so. The only man he ever told the whole unvarnished story to was the old Voivode Mishitch, who was fascinated and laughed a lot. Later the grey suits in the Foreign Office would take an interest, but that was a few years off.

Here Strutt's diary comes to a close.

Chapter Thirty-Two

What Happened Next

In May 1919, three weeks after Strutt left them, the Imperial Family moved to the Villa Prangins (now called Prangins Castle.) This was a large and comfortable chateau at the very western tip of Switzerland. Here their sixth child was born, a boy they named Rudolf. The birth went well and Karl and Zita hoped to make Prangins their home. Unfortunately, the Swiss government couldn't quite settle to having the fugitive Emperor of Austria in their country. They feared the potential for all manner of troubles, so a more permanent home would have to be found.

Lt Colonel and Mrs Strutt returned to England where they were very pleased to discover he had been invited to join the secret Special Reserve of Officers known as 'Class X'. This was a great honour and he was delighted to accept. The idea was that a whole officer structure could spring from the woodwork, so to speak, if the Germans ever rose again. This was a safeguard set up by members of the military who worried that the terms of the Treaty of Versailles were too stringent for the Germans to stomach. They were right. Strutt was also given command of one of his regiment's battalions as he expected. Their new home would be Edinburgh, a city he and Florrie had enjoyed before the war and where they had many friends.

This posting lasted barely a year. Strutt's talents were needed elsewhere. In 1920, he was made High Commissioner of Danzig by the League of Nations. This was a new appointment. The Free City of Danzig was created in November 1920 in accordance with the terms of the Treaty of Versailles. This region, now called by its Polish name Gdansk, was to remain separate from Germany and also separate from the newly-resurrected nation of Poland, but it was not an independent state. It was a protectorate of the League of Nations.

The problem had been that while Germany had claimed the region as part of its former provinces of Pomerania and West Prussia – and indeed the population was mainly German – Poland needed access to the sea. Therefore, the solution was to remove the region from the power of both. This was one of those solutions that looked good on paper, but don't work in practice. Danzig was a snake pit from its first day and needed a strong hand to control it. Strutt did his best.

The following February 1921, while Strutt and his wife were on leave skiing in St. Moritz with friends – among whom was Archduke Eugen the Emperor's brother – he received a message that a *person* was coming to see him. This turned out to be Lt von Seedak with a verbal message from the Emperor. Would Strutt come to him immediately at Prangins? He was needed. Strutt left that afternoon. Here follows a most extraordinary story which got Strutt into very hot water.

The Emperor Karl had decided to make the attempt to regain the throne of Hungary. To do this, he first needed to prepare the ground with France and England. His brother-on-law, Prince Sixtus, was once again employed as emissary.

After listening carefully to Sixtus, Monsieur Brand, the French Prime Minister said that if Karl managed to get back to Hungary and proclaim himself King, thus presenting a faite accompli, neither France nor England would make the slightest opposition. He might even find that Italy was in accord as well. M. Briand did not think any of the Allies would be much interested. This was almost certainly doubtful at best.

Karl, now thinking there was all to play for, asked Strutt to go to Paris to confirm this statement with Prince Sixtus and to do whatever else he deemed necessary to prepare his way to the Hungarian throne. This was an outrageous request to make to a serving British officer and Strutt knew it. Nevertheless, he volunteered to undertake it. At this point, he must have thought he was merely going on a fact-finding mission for a friend.

Afterwards, trying to cover his back, Strutt admitted in a written account to the Foreign Office that he went to Paris solely to interview Prince Sixtus. At his house in the Rue de Varenne, however, he also found Sixtus' great friend Marechal Lyautey[1] present. Lyautey was most

---

1. Louis Hubert Gonzalve Lyautry 1854-1934 of French colonial fame. After serving in Indochina and Madagascar, he became the first French Resident-General in Morocco 1912-25. Minister of War briefly in 1917. In 1921 he was made a Marechal of France. Dubbed the 'French Empire Builder.'

anxious that the Hungarian coup d'etat should be brought off as soon as possible, but there was the problem that the Emperor did not own a passport.

Sixtus came up with a plan. He asked Strutt to see if he could cross the Austrian-Swiss frontier at Martinsbruck, Lower Engadine without showing his passport. If he managed it, the Emperor might be able to do the same. Strutt wrote in his account to the Foreign Office that 'as this suited a long-standing engagement of his to meet Count Czernin at Landeck, he consented.' This was certainly ridiculous. He also wrote that 'I saw Sixtus again that evening and received from him, I believed, a passport for the Emperor.' Not true.

Strutt went to St. Moritz, told Florrie he would be back in a couple of days and went by train to Tarasp, where he took a sleigh to Remus, a tiny Swiss frontier village in the Lower Engadine. As an alibi in case he was caught and questioned, he had a letter from a friend in his pocket betting him 5000 francs that he could not cross the frontier without showing his passport. What was he thinking?

That night, from his lodging at Remus, he then crossed the frontier on foot by means of the steep rocks above the left bank of the River Inn and returned by the same route a few hours later. He met no one. He decided the climb was so rigorous and unpleasant in the dark, it was suitable only for a practiced mountaineer. The Emperor would never manage it.

In his account again to the Foreign Office, Strutt folded in numerous disclaimers stating that he had begged the Emperor not to attempt to regain his throne until the following year, but despite his pleas the Emperor had been determined to start. 'He preferred not to tell me the date of his departure or the route.'

On his return to London, Strutt saw Colonel Twiss of the War Office and Mr Cadogan of the Foreign Office and 'gave them as much information as I could.' Afterwards, Strutt says he wrote again to the Emperor Karl imploring him not to start out and received an acknowledgment of receipt of his letter. Here is a man covering his tracks.

What actually happened as the Empress herself confessed many years later, was that Strutt had indeed gone to Paris to meet with Prince Sixtus, but in attendance at the meeting besides Marechal Lyautey, were Maurice Paleologue, a former ambassador to St. Petersburg and one of the foremost diplomatists of the day and M. Briand, the French Prime

Minister himself. Strutt took over and personally negotiated on the Habsburg's behalf. So, Strutt had not only been up to his neck in it, he had been in it right to the top.[2] For a serving British officer, this was surely a court martial offence!

Nothing daunted, thinking he had got conditional permission from the French and the British, the Emperor Karl continued with his plans to regain the throne of Hungary. A meticulous plan was made and executed. The route over the mountains reconnoitred by Strutt proved not to be practical, so another way was found.

On 24 March, 1921, with trusted aides, Karl made his way first to Salzburg and then to Vienna where he stayed with Count Thomas Erododi. Next, a taxi driven by a faithful chauffeur to his grandmother, Archduchess Maria Theresa, carried Erododi and him to the Hungarian border at Sinnersdort. Here he produced an English passport in the name of Mr William Codo of the British Red Cross. Where this passport came from was soon to be of major interest at the Foreign Office in London.

Most unfortunately, this bid for restoration was a failure as was his second bid. Collectively they are known as the Easter Restoration. On Easter Saturday, with only two aides, the Emperor in secret astounded Admiral Horthy, who had just been elected Regent for Hungary, by appearing out of the blue at the Royal Palace where he was staying. He was confident that his mere presence would be enough to secure power.

The Admiral, who owed his rise in life to the emporer's grace, had assured him time and again that he would hand over the throne immediately if the emperor ever asked and indeed he said it again, but this time he threw in a caveat; if he did hand over, the allied armies of the newly formed Czech and Yugoslav republics, formed out of the old Hungary, would immediately invade. They feared a return to monarchy and would resist it. Karl did not agree. His informants told him he still had significant support in the country. This was probably true, but it wasn't the whole story. At that time, Hungary was a powder keg of revolutionaries of all sorts needing a very strong hand to control it. The Emperor was not that man. Horthy knew that disaster would follow a restoration from inside as well as outside the country. He wrote later that 'these moments were the most difficult of his entire life.' In the end, he persuaded the Emperor that the best plan was for

---

2. Gordon Brook-Shepherd's *The Last Empress*, 1991.

him to return to Switzerland to gather armed support from his Austrian followers so that he could march on Vienna in force, while Horthy gathered support in Hungary. 'Within weeks you will again be ruler of the twin capitals', he cajoled him.

This was all nonsense, of course. Faced with such a weak sovereign, Horthy had no intention of giving up power – for his country or himself. Monarchy was finished. Karl had made two fatal mistakes. The first was that he had entered the capital without even a company of loyal soldiers behind him. The second was to turn around and leave with only a few thin promises in his hand. Karl felt angry with Horthy, he had been assured that the great powers and everyone else would not oppose a restoration once it was a fait accompli . He also believed in his heart that the Hungarian people truly wanted him to return.

Gordon Brook-Shepherd opined that if Strutt had been with him on the first bid, Horthy might have capitulated or they would have immediately gone around to the Budapest garrison and roused the men to fall in behind their anointed King. Strutt would have had them running for their rifles and overthrowing the impudent Regent within the hour. Alas, the Emperor Karl was not such a man. He was exhausted from the effort of confronting Horthy.

Some months later, in October 1921, with Zita accompanying him, he returned with a second restoration bid. This was a larger enterprise with troops. This attempt might have succeeded but for the treachery and betrayal of men he mistakenly thought were loyal officers. Also, it has to be said, it failed because Karl simply did not have the iron will required to bring the enterprise to a successful conclusion. The whole affair was a farce of misunderstandings, ludicrous skirmishes and muddled thinking. When he saw his countrymen shooting at each other and actually killing each other in a sporadic fight along a provincial railway outside of Budapest, he was shocked into staying his hand. He had actually believed he could seize back the crown without shedding any blood. He thought a show of force would be enough. He did not have the heart to continue if it meant his people would be hurt. Admiral Horthy had won. In fact, this traitor to his Emperor, but not to his country, remained Regent of Hungary right up until he was thrown out by the Germans during the Second World War.

Chapter Thirty-Three

Summer 1922 to late Spring 1923

As glad as he was that the Emperor's second restoration bid had failed, Horthy shrank from putting his sovereign under arrest. Here was a problem: Karl still had considerable support in the Hungary and elsewhere, but he lacked enough intelligence and force of character to become ruler, let alone a good one. It was a stalemate. He could not be arrested and he could not be allowed to go free.

In the end, the French solved the problem. They proposed that the Portuguese island of Madeira would be the ideal spot for the Habsburg retreat and the Portuguese government agreed with the proviso that the maintenance of the family would not fall on them.

Here was another impasse. The British Lord Curzon did his best to secure an income for the Imperial Family. He first suggested that the 'inheriting states' – Poland, Yugoslavia, Czechoslovakia and Romania should club together to provide a modest but decent pension. They all ingenuously reneged for various reasons, mainly that 'he was rich enough already.' Curzon then tackled the Allies – Britain, France, Italy and even Japan. Telling them it was a matter of practical politics; a settled Emperor would be less likely to try again for another restoration bid. The British Treasury turned him down; the French and Italian governments side-stepped the issue. The Japanese said nothing. Curzon did not know at that time that the Czech, Polish, French and Austrian Government's had already confiscated all the fixed assets of the dynasty and frozen its bank and investment holdings abroad and they would concede nothing.

Meanwhile, in late October 1922, Karl and Zita were taken under guard to the Tihany monastery on Lake Balaton, the largest lake in Central Europe. This monastery had been built in the eighteenth century on a spectacularly beautiful promontory reaching into the lake half way up its western side. The monks greeted them with great friendship and courtesy as did the local people who pressed them with flowers and smiles. They could have been on holiday instead of being prisoners. Count Esterhazy,

Zita's old nanny and a few servants were with them. It was as all very pleasant as one sun- filled day followed another. Their Majesties did their best to keep their spirits up and not worry about the future. They were so grateful that their children were still safely at Wartegg. That was one worry less. One morning Zita, somewhat flustered, announced that she was pregnant again. It was not the best time.

She spent her days knitting and reading and dreaming in the sunshine. It was a delightful situation. Facing the monastery was the glory of Lake Balaton, the largest fresh water lake in central Europe. Just breathing the air and watching the clouds changing their shapes filled them with peace and hope. All this was wonderful enough, but at the rear they overlooked yet another lovely lake. This one, Tihany Lake, was tiny in comparison to the other, but perfect for boating and swimming. Karl and Esterhazy enjoyed themselves there. It wasn't too cold. Once, they visited the local school to give out prizes and receive more bouquets.

Finally, in November came news. They were to go to Madeira. No other information was given. Indeed, there was no other information. The Allies had not yet agreed a plan as to where they would live or on what allowance. On 31 October, they were taken by train to Baja on the Duna River where a small naval flotilla was waiting on the Danube to transport them downstream to Orsova, which was situated just before the Iron Gates. There, by car and train, they made their way to Galantz where they expected to meet a British cruiser. The whole trip was surreal. At every stop there were crowds of people thrilled to see them, waving flags and saluting. It was like a festival – just the opposite of what they were actually experiencing. At Galantz, they received word there wasn't sufficient water in the Danube at that point to accommodate HMS Cardiff, so it was awaiting them instead at Salina on the Black Sea. A Romanian steamer would transport them there.

At Galantz, the newly married Hunyadys joined them, relieving Count Esterhazy to return to his estates. There were many tears. Esterhazy didn't want to leave, but the Emperor had charged him with many messages and instructions, most of them of no use at all.

The Hunyadys had brought much need provisions of clothes for them both and a new pair of dreadful American shoes for the Emperor, but at least they fitted. That afternoon, they received joyous news. A telegram came from Colonel Strutt in London saying that all was well with their children. It was their first news in eighteen days and proved that the Colonel had not deserted them. This was comforting.

Once on the cruiser, their first stop was Constantinople, but they weren't allowed to leave the ship. They ran into a storm which laid Karl and Zita very low with sea sickness. Finally they reached Gibraltar on 15 November, but were again not allowed to go ashore. Even the Hunyadys were forbidden. The Governor sent a beautiful basket of flowers and fruit to the Empress, instead of the expected invitation to visit. (London had given strict instructions.)

After that, they took to the Atlantic in heavy seas. The three day journey to Madeira was atrocious. Another storm hit them and followed them nearly all the way. Karl was dreadfully ill. At journey's end on 19 November 1921, they discovered to their dismay that still nothing had been decided about how and where they were to live. The captain was himself upset. How could he leave these exalted persons beached, as it were, in the middle of the Atlantic? London had no answers.

So it was that when Karl and Zita and their entourage stepped ashore at Funchal, they had nothing but what they brought with them. Her jewels which were of almost incalculable value had been taken to Switzerland ten days before they left Eckartsau in March. Sadly, and almost unbelievably, they had fallen victim to a confidence trickster named Bruno Steiner, an Austrian businessman who had once been Consul General in Genoa. Somehow, this man had persuaded the Emperor to not only to create him a Baron, but to also give him access to the jewels which were in the safe-keeping of the Swiss National Bank in Zurich. Steiner promised faithfully to sell only some of the lesser pieces to allow the Emperor much needed ready cash. That, of course, was the last they saw of the jewels.[1]

Their party now was a small one. The Hunyadys were with them, along with their personal servants, but no one else. Indeed, seeing the unprecedented straits the Imperial Couple were in, the Hunyadys removed themselves after Christmas to return to Austria to see what help they could find for them.

For the moment they were ensconced in the Villa Victoria made available by Reid's Palace Hotel, the premier hotel on the island. It was

---

1. In his book *The Last Empress*, Gordon Brook-Shepherd called this the biggest heist of the century, but few knew of it.

the annex, but it enjoyed the same glorious view over the Atlantic as the hotel itself. They could have been happy there, but unfortunately, they only had funds for a few more weeks lodging.

At this point, after the rigours of travel and being unsettled, the Emperor became unwell again. Despite this, Zita, using an alias, was forced to leave him to go to Switzerland. She had received word that her son Robert was to have a small operation and was asking for her. Also, she needed to see if she could salvage some money to keep them all.

Fortunately, her little boy made a good recovery, but there was little she could do about the financial problem. Her family was as generous as they could be, but they themselves were having difficulties. She had to face the fact that the entire bulk of the Habsburg's vast wealth was irretrievably gone. The Swiss also took the opportunity to reiterate that her presence was not wanted. In this debacle, there was only one consolation. All the children would be following her to Madeira within days. The family would be united again after all the worry and upset.

Now there was a new problem. With the addition of seven young children and three nannies into the establishment, it was more urgent that ever to find a suitable place for them to live which was more spacious and less expensive that Reids Hotel annex. They were not short of offers, but they were all too expensive. Colonel Strutt, in his last recorded message to them, wrote of an offer from a Miss E. Lindon who had a property she was willing to let to them, but that proved too expensive as well.

At last, a local Portuguese banker who owned a lot of property on the island, produced the answer. He offered the Emperor his villa above the bay rent-free. This was enormously appreciated by the desperate Imperial Couple and despite it being only partially furnished, they accepted with alacrity.

In early February the children joined them and the family moved to the Villa in the middle of February 1922, a time of year that the sun only shone near the shoreline. 'The densely wooded hills surrounded the villa high above were habitually wreathed in a damp mist which only the midsummer heat burned away. For anyone with a weak chest it was a death trap.'[2]

_____

2. Ibid.

An Austrian maid, who had joined the Imperial Couple some weeks before at Christmas, wrote a description of their situation to her family.

'Down below, the sun shines every day and when it rains, it is not for long, but up here we have had only three warm days. The rest has been rain, fog and damp all the time. There is no electric light, water only on the first floor and down in the kitchen. Our only fuel is green wood which of course smokes all the time. We wash only with cold water and soap...The house is so damp that it all smells of mildew and the mist penetrates everywhere.

The only means of communication are cars and ox-carts which we cannot afford, or else a mountain railway. To go to Funchal and back on foot takes all day. The poor emperor...can have no meat in the evenings, only vegetables and puddings, which upsets us all very much. He don't (sic) mind. I don't miss it, but we really do not have enough to eat...

'I am writing without Their Majesties' knowledge. I just cannot bear that these two innocent people should be left so long in this completely inadequate house. Someone ought to protest! Sometimes we do get very low and depressed, but when we see how patiently Their Majesties accept all these ills, we carry on again courageously.'[3]

It was the long walk to Funchal on March 9th that finished Karl in the end. He had gaily set out to buy some toys for Charles Louis who would be four years old the following day. He declared he didn't need an overcoat as the day was mild. On the way back, climbing up from the sunshine into the mists, he caught a cold. This turned to pneumonia and three weeks later on 1 April 1922 he was gone, a prematurely grey man of only thirty five years. The world had been too hard a place for this good and well-meaning, but fragile man. Zita, who had been a tower of strength throughout his illness was now completely alone and eight months pregnant with her eighth child. On top of this, two of her children were down with pneumonia, Robert had a gastric infection and most of the staff had the influenza.

---

3. Ibid.

They buried Karl, the last Emperor of Austria, four days later in the church near the villa. It was a pauper's funeral with no horse-drawn golden catafalque , no motor vehicle. Instead the coffin was carried on a simple two-wheeled hand cart by the men of his modest household. Nevertheless, as if sensing that history was being made, a large crowd of interested bystanders came up from Funchal to peer at the suffering family. Zita, the tearless widow, with her three eldest children none of whom lost their composure, deeply impressed all with her warmth and calm. What was to become of this poor, stranded family now?

Chapter Thirty-Four

A New Life

In May 1922, with time pressing, Zita and her children were rescued by her brother-in-law, King Alfonso of Spain. It was a close run thing. Most of the Central Powers – Austria, Germany and Italy – were not happy to see her leave Madeira, fearing a future third Hasburg restoration, but they recognised something had to be done. She was about to give birth again.

The Infante Isabel was sent to Funchal to collect the forlorn family with their nannies and servants and take them to Cadiz. They were then taken by train to Madrid and installed at the Pardo Palace where Zita gave birth to her third daughter, Elisabeth. Despite everything she had been through – bereavement, the exhausting journey, both Zita and the baby came out of the ordeal healthy and strong.

The Pardo Palace was not deemed suitable for a long stay, so in June they removed to the Palacio Uribarren overlooking the Bay of Biscay near the Basque fishing village of Lequietio in the north of Spain. This was ideal – tranquil, out of the way, the perfect setting for a young family to grow up. Even better, the village folk of Lequietio took them to their hearts. The children always remembered their years there with fondness. They stayed six years.

After that, due to political unrest and threats against Alfonso's throne which he was to lose two years later, in 1929 they moved to Brussels. It was time for Otto to attend university and Zita had chosen the University of Louvain. Her reasons were twofold: safety and stability. Above all Zita's flock of fledglings needed to live in safety. As it happened, her first cousin, Princess Elisabeth of Bavaria, was the wife of King Albert of the Belgians and Belgium was stable. They would be safe there until Hitler's rise in Germany a few years later made it imperative that they move again.

In the meantime, just after Karl's second failed restoration bid in October 1921, Strutt was in trouble back in Britain. The Foreign Office wanted to know how and where had the non-existent Mr William Codo of the British Red Cross obtained his English passport to enter Hungary?

As we know, some months before, Strutt had barely survived the Foreign Office enquiry into his dealings with the French authorities in aid of Karl's Easter Restoration bid. The Foreign Office had insisted on severe disciplinary action for his 'ambitious meddling', but he was saved by the jealous fury of the War Office who were outraged at the thought that 'civilians', that is the Foreign Office, should attempt to censure a British officer!

This time, the Foreign Office was after blood. They knew full well Strutt must have organised the passport from his office as High Commissioner of Danzig, but there was no proof. They were powerless to express their wrath, but Strutt felt the heat on his back nevertheless.

This is no doubt the reason he abruptly resigned from the secret Special Reserve of Officers and the reason why when his time came to retire from the army at age 55 in 1929, the Foreign Office denied his request to retire with the title of full Colonel. His Habsburg adventure had not been forgiven or forgotten. He knew he had been lucky to get away so easily, but it hurt. The army had been his life.

Strutt was not down for long. In 1922, he became second in command of a party under General Bruce for the assault on the North Col of Everest. George Mallory was a member of this team which set out without oxygen and reached 26,800 feet. (Eighteen months later, Mallory tried again and this time famously died in 1924.) Strutt loved the challenge of mountain climbing and continued to do so for some years.

He later became editor of the Alpine Club journal, the very respected organ of the highly prestigious Alpine Club in London. Eventually, he became its President as well. By that time, he had acquired a reputation for being a crotchety and arrogant old man. He had written numerous articles and gave a famous speech in which he contended that climbing with oxygen was unsportsmanlike and that using crampons and such-like was for sissies. Real men, he asserted, managed without! Perhaps it was true in his day, but times had changed. Many members protested.

In 1939, when war was declared again, he offered his services to the War Office as an officer and former member of Class X and was refused. He raged over this as he knew he could be of real help on the Eastern Front. The terrain hadn't changed! The letter had thanked him for his invaluable service in the last war, but explained they were only taking men up to the age of 45.

Like all former officers who had wanted to re-enlist, Strutt was frustrated and angry at the situation, but there was nothing to be done. He and Florrie continued to live near Edinburgh as they had done since 1921. They had a good life together. They travelled regularly to France, sometimes they went into Italy, never into Austria. The old friends had mostly died after what was gloriously called The Great War and for those few who hadn't he preferred to remember them as they were – strong and tall and wonderfully amusing.

Lieutenant Colonel Edward Lisle Strutt died peacefully on 7 July 1948 with Florrie by his side. He was 74. Rescuing the Imperial Habsburg family had been the highlight of his life and he had no regrets.

Note

Towards the end of his life, Otto von Habsburg, President of the International Pan European Union and Member of the European Union for Bavaria, was asked by a journalist if he wasn't disappointed that the British Royal Family had not helped his family after the Great War? 'Oh, but they did,' he replied. 'They sent us Colonel Strutt.'

Envoi

Zita lived on. When the Nazis invaded Belgium in 1939, she and her family became refugees. They fled to the Spanish border, then to Portugal where the US government granted them exit visas to New York. After many vicissitudes, they settled in Canada. Money was very tight. At one stage she was reduced to creating salads and spinach dishes from her garden, but her sons grew up one by one and shouldered the financial burden.

In 1952, with so many weddings of her children taking place in Europe, she moved back. First to Luxembourg to look after her aging mother, the dear old Duchess of Parma and finally to the Castle at Zizers, Switzerland, which had become a Convent. Here she was invited to stay as a permanent guest by the Bishop of Chur, who was an old friend. This was her last residence.

For many years, she travelled Europe to see her family. In 1988 she contracted pneumonia and spent some of the autumn and winter bedridden. Finally early in March 1989, she called Otto and told him she was dying. The family gathered and took turns staying with her until she died on March 14. She was ninety-six years old, the indomitable matriarch of thirty-three grandchildren.

In Vienna on 1 April 1989 very early in the morning people walking to work were amazed to see the funeral cortege of their last Empress being driven down the main thoroughfare by four black horses with plumes. It was such a surprise to most of them; so few remembered her or anything about her. She was laid to rest, as was fitting, in the Imperial crypt under the Capuchin church. She had asked that her heart be placed with her husband's at Muri Abbey, Switzerland.

The Emperor Karl's body still lies on Madeira in a chapel especially dedicated to him. He has since been canonised for his role as a peacemaker and for putting his Christian faith and his love for his countrymen before his own worldly considerations. Her canonisation is pending.

Obituary

From *The Thistle*, official regimental journal of the
Royal Scots Fusiliers, October 1948

LIEUTENANT-COLONEL E. L. STRUTT, C.B.E., DSO

It is with deep regret that we record the death of Lieutenant-Colonel
E.L. Strutt. He joined the 3rd (Militia) Battalion in the nineties and
served with it in the South African War. He took part in the 1914–18
War (not with the Regiment) and held many important high diplomatic
appointments. For his services he was awarded the C.B.E. and the
D.S.O., the Croix de Guerre with four palms, Chevalier and Officer of
the Legion of Honour, Chevalier of Order of Leopold, Belgian Croix de
Guerre and Palm. Officer of Star of Roumania, 1914 Star and Clasp.

In 1920 he was High Commissioner of Danzig.

Lieutenant-Colonel Strutt was well known as a leading mountain
climber and in 1922 was Second-in-Command of the Mount Everest
expedition. We would express to his widow our deep sympathy in her
loss.

The Right Hon. L.S. Amery writes in *The Times of 13th July:*

"May an old colleague of Colonel Strutt's both on active service
and as a mountaineer, add a few lines to your obituary notice? In
the record of his military and quasi-diplomatic services something
should, I think, be said of his part in 1916-17 as Field-Marshal
Milne's principal liaison officer with French Headquarters at
Salonika, no easy task, especially when dealing with so arbitrary a
personality as General Sarrail, but most successfully accomplished.
Nor does your notice refer to a subsequent action of his in which he
always looked back with special satisfaction. In March 1919, as an

officer of the Allied Council in Vienna, acting with great initiative and resolution, he rescued the Austrian Imperial Family from the revolutionary mob, commandeered a train and himself took them safely into Switzerland."

For ten years, from 1927 to 1937, he edited the *Alpine Journal*, bringing to his task a scholarly and critical analysis.

References

Alpine Journal: Edward Lisle Strutt 'Pugnacious Defender of Emperor Charles', (*The Monarchist*, July 2008). Also Strutt's Valedictory Address 1968.

Article E.L. Strutt, 'A Superiority Complex' in *Mirrors of the Cliff*, ed. J. Perrin, (Diadem, 1983),

Birch, Nigel *No Sideshow: The British Contribution to the Allied Victory in the Balkans, September 1918* (UK: Niroad Publications: 2018).

Birdwell, Robert. *Morocco Under Colonial Rule: French administration of Tribal Areas 1912–56*. Routledge 1973.

Bourne, J.M. *Who's Who in WW1*. New York. Taylor & Francis. E-library 2002. Re: Otto Bauer.

Bradford, Lt Col Lord a.k.a. Orlando Bridgeman. www.military-history.fandom.com

Brook-Shepherd, Gordon. 'Obituary of Zita of Bourbon-Parma', *New York Times* 2 April 1989. *The Last Habsburg* (1968). Weidenfeld and Nicolson, *Victims of Sarajevo* (Harper Collins, 1984). *The Last Empress* (Harper Collins, 1991). *The Uncrowned Emperor* (Hambledon and London, 2003).

Bryant, Arthur, *Jackets of Green: A Study of the History, Philosophy and Character of the Rifle Brigade* (Collins 1972).

Clayton, Anthony. *Histoire de l'Armee Francaise e Aftique 1930–1962* (Albin M. Michele, 1996)

Daggett, Mabel Potter *Marie of Roumania*. (New York. George H. Doran & Co. 1926)

Dowling, Timothy C, Eastern Front from the International Encyclopaedia of the First World War 1914–18 online.

Duke of Parma, Charles II *Encyclopedia Britannica* 11th ed.

Dutton D.J., 'The Balkan Campaign and French War Aims in the Great War'. *English History Review* Vol. 94.

Encyclopedia Britannica online Ed: Leo Amery 1873–1955.

Esterhazy, Court Alexnder, *Encyclopedia Britannica*, Esterhazy family. 2008.

Falls, C. Military Operations Macedonia: from the Outbreak of war to the spring of 1919. Re: The Allied Army of the Orient and others.

Gambetta-Jounet, General. Wikipedia.

Gelardi, Julia (2005) *Born to Rule*. (London, St. Martin's Griffen, 2008).

Gilbert, Martin. *First World War* (Atlas 1970).

Godsey, William D. *Aristocratic Redout*: *The Austro-Hungarian Foreign Office on the eve of WW1*, regarding James Forgach 1870–1935, second section chief of the Imperial Foreign Ministry 1913–1917 (Purdue UP 1999).

Gooch, John *The Italian Army and the First World War* (Cambridge University Press 2014), regarding General cardona's methods.

Greenhaigh, Elizabeth *The French Army and the First World War* (Cambridge University Press 2014).

Halpern, Paul G. Troubridge, Sir Ernest Charles Thomas (1862–1926) *Oxford Dictionary of National Biography 2004.*

Hevesy, William. Postscript on the Sixtus Affair. *Foreign Affairs Magazine* Vol 21. 3 April 1943. Published by Council of Foreign Relations.

Hoffmann, Robert, 'The British Military Representative in Vienna 1919 in *The Slavonic and Eastern European Review* 52 (1974). Regarding Sir Thomas Montgomery-Cuninghame, 10th baronet.

Howell, PA, Bridges, General Sir Tom Bridges (1871–1939), *Australian Dictionary of Biography.* Australian National University.

Imaging Everest, Royal Geographical Society.org

Infante Alfonso of Spain. Wikipedia

James, Williams Jr. 'The Austro-Hungarian Decision for War in July 1914' in *Essays on WW1: Origins and Prisoners of War* (New York 1983).

Jukes, Geoffrey *The First World War. The Eastern Front 1914–1918* (Osprey 2002).

Jukes, Geoffrey *The First World War. The Eastern Front 1914–1918* (Osprey 2002).

Jukes, Geoffrey: Essential History Series. The First World War: The Eastern Front 1914–19.

Karl Renner 1870–1950. *Encyclopedia Britannia 1922* and Wikipedia.

Karolyi, Count. *Encyclopedia Britannica.*

Keegan, John *The First World War* (Hutchinson, 1998)

Kinsky, Count Karl, www.military-history.fandom.com. He was the brother of Maritschy Czernin and lover of Jenny Churchill.

Koch, John *Daisy Princess of Piess 1873–1943: A Discovery* (W. John Kock, 2003).

Low, Alfred. D, The Anchluss Movement: 1918–1938, in the *Canadian Review of Studies.* 3 November 1926.

Magocsi, Paul Robert *Historical Atlas of Central Europe* (University of Washington Press 2002).

Marck, Miroslav. Festetics de Toina. Geology. EU. Online.

Maria Pavlovna of Russia A Princess in Exile. Viking, 1932.

Mishitch, Voivode, in A Balkin Capital, *The North American Review.* Vol 213. May 1921.

Obituary of Archduke Felix of Austria, *The Times*, 20 September 2011.

Obituary of Lt Col Edward Lisle Strutt, *The Thistle*, Regimental magazine of The Royal Scots Fusilliers. October 1948.

Obituary of the Empress Zita. 'A Century in the Life of Empress Zita', *Daily Telegraph* 16 March 1989.

Palmer, Alan, *Victory 1918* (Weidenfeld & Nicolson 1998) Re, General George Miles. (Milne wrote a book, but did not mention Strutt).

Pounds, N.J.G. *A Historical Geography of Europe* (Cambridge University Press 1993).

Records of the Royal Scots Regiment. (Very little here. The Records office in London seems to have taken a direct hit during WW2.)

Sakmyster, Thomas L. *Hungary's Admiral on Gorseback*. East European Monograph, (Boulder co. 1994).

Sakmyster, Thomas, 'From Habsburg Admiral to Hungarian Regent. The Political Metamorphosis of Miklos Horthy 1918–1921. *East European Quarterly* 17.2 (1993).

Strutt, Lt Col Edward Lisle. 'Three Months of 1919'. Archive at Windsor Castle.

Szchenyi, Gabriele (Yella). www.geni.com and www.de.rodovid.org

The National Archive Kew, Minute Sheet regarding E.L. Strutt's War Records. (Nothing much here except a brief hand-written list of where he was sent during his army career.)

Tucker, Spencer C. WWI: The Definitive Encyclopaedia and document collection, 2014.

Tuckman, Barbara, *The Guns of August* (Random House, 1962). Re. General Berthelot.

Tunstell, Graydon A. Jr. *'Austria-Hungary and the Brusilov Offnesive.'* 2008.

Tunstell, Graydon A. Jr. 'Austria-Hungary' in *The Origin of World War I*. (Cambridge University Press 2003). Re. Count von Hoyos, *chef de cabinet of the Imperial Foreign Ministry 1912–17* and Count Leopold Berthold.

Vincent, C. Paul. Mises Daily Articles: The Blockade and Attempted Starvation of Germany from The Politics of Hunger: Allied Blockade of Germany 1915–1919. (Ohio University Press 1985).

Principal Characters

Archduchess Maria Josefa. Mother of Emperor Karl. Born Princess Maria Josefa of Saxony.

Archduchess Maria Theresia. (1862–1933). Aunt to Empress Zita and step-grandmother to Emperor Karl.

Archduke Maximillian Eugen. Brother of Emperor Karl. Wife Franziska Hohenlohe.

Ashmore, Lance Corporal. Military policeman with York and Lancaster Regiment stationed at Flume.

Babington, Lieutenant General James (1843–1936). Commander in Chief of 23rd Div, part of Kitchener's army.

Barclay, Sir George, British Minister, Bucharest.

Bauer, Otto. Prime Minister of the new Republic of Austria.

von Bellegarde, Countess Gabriella. (1890–1945). Friend and lady in waiting to Empress Zita.

Berthelot, General Mathias (1861–1931). Chief of General Staff under Joffre. Commander of French Military Mission in Romanian Campaign. In 1916 he was put in charge of retraining and reorganizing the Romanian army which was a decisive success.

Borckhardt. Nephew of M. Buchard, Minister of the Swiss Legation.

Bourbon-Parma, Prince Sixtus. Brother of Empress Zita. Belgian Officer in the First World War (1886–1934). Emperor Karl used Prince Sixtus as a go-between in his attempted peace negotiation with France behind the back of Germany in 1917.

Braganza, Duke of. Brother of Duchess of Parma and uncle to Empress Zita. Pretender to the throne of Portugal. Commanded an Austrian Cavalry Corps in WW1.

Bridges, Lieutenant General Sir Tom. (1887–1939) late commander of the British Salonika Force. Now removed to Constantinople.

Burchard. Minister, Swiss Legation.

Butler, Mr. British Food Commissioner for Hungary, Austria and Yugoslavia.

Chretien, General. Commander of the Allied Troops of Occupation, Bulgaria

Cuninghame, Lieutenant Colonel Sir Thomas Montgomery-Cuninghame, Bt. (1872–1932). Head of British Military Mission in Vienna and Prague.

Czernin, Count Ottokar von. 'Kary', (1872–1932). Former Imperial Foreign Minister of Austria-Hungary. Married to Maritschy Kinsky.

de Esperay, General Francet. June 1918 succeeded Guillaumat as Supreme Commander Armee en Orient.

des Graz (1860–1940). British Minister, Bucharest.

de Fontaney. French Minister, Belgrade.

de Lobit, General Commander 3rd *Groupement, Armée d'Orient* 'the East Albanian show' during the last offensive.

Dosse, Lieutenant Colonel. A mountaineering friend of Strutt's in Macedonia and Serbia. Made full Colonel and Chief of Staff eventually. 1918 Deputy Chief of Staff, Armée d'Orient.

Emperor Karl (b. 1887). Slight, lovable, intelligent, brave, but weak.

Empress Zita, born a Bourbon-Parma 1892. Huge strength of character.

Esterhazy, Count Alexander. One of the Emperor's chamberlain. Hungarian.

Expert-Besancon, General. Chief of Staff, *Armée d'Orient* under General Henrys.

Festetics, Princess Mary, née Douglas-Hamilton. Sister of 12th Duke of Hamilton. Married first, the Crown Prince of Monaco, secondly Prince Tazilo Festetics. Six Festetics children. Three daughters: Princess Mary Furstenberg, Princess Alexandra Hohenlohe, Princes Kila Festhetics.

Festetics, Prince Taszilo. (1850–1933) her husband.

Festetics, George. (1882–1941). Their son, a soldier and diplomat. Spent the last two years on Staff of Italian Front.

Fresan, General. Chief of the French General Staff 1919.

Galliera, Duke of. Infante Alfonso of Spain. Husband of Princess Beatrice of Coburg (sister of Queen Marie of Romania).

Guillaumat, General Adolf. December. 1917–June 1918, succeeded Sarrail as Supreme Commander *Armée Allies en Orient.*

Hamilton, Duchess of. Sister-on-law of Princess Mary Festetics and a Friend of Strutt's.

Henrys, General Paul-Prosper KCB. French Commander Armée d'Orient from 31 December 1917. This was the French army in Macedonia, which had become international.

Henrys' ADCs: Lieutenant Prince Paul Murat (1893–1964) Col. du Tilly.

von Hoetzandorff (1852–1925). Late Chief of the Austrian General Staff. Not a success.

Hunyady, Count Joseph. (1873–1942). Steward to the Imperial household and confident of the Emperor. First cousin of Maritschy Czernin. Fiance of Gabriella von Bellegarde.

Jouinot-Gambetta, a great friend of Strutt's. Brilliant cavalry man. Served in French *Armée d'Orient.*

Karolyl, Mihaly, Late Prime Minister of Hungary and a terrible scoundrel.

Kinsky, Count Karl. (1858–1919). Brother of Maritschy Czernin.

Leodoffski, Colonel Count. One of the Emperor's chamberlain. Weak, incapable, but charming.

Lonyay, Princess. (Princess Stephanie of Belgium, late widow of Crown Prince Rudolf von Habsburg.) (1864–1945). Wife of Prince Lonyay.

Mensdorff, Count Albert von Mensdorff-Pouilly-Dietrichstein. 1861–1945. Austro-Hungarian ambassador to London. Highly respected.

Milne, General George. Commander in Chief of British Macedonian Front based at Salonika from 1916.

Mishitch, Voivode. Commander in Chief Royal Serbian Army. A great man. Highly respected.

Napier, Colonel. British Military attaché in Sofia.

Parker. Second in command, but real organiser of the British Food Commission, Vienna.

Parma, Duchess of. Born the Infanra Maria Antonia of Portugal. Second wife of Robert I, Duke of Parma who died in 1907. Mother of Empress Zita and eleven others.

Patey, General. Commander 2nd Groupement (16th Colonial Div. and the 30th Metropolitan) French.

Paulier. Head of Intelligence of 'Groupmement Patey'. Held similar position at GHQ Salonika.

Pless, Princess Daisy of. Fading Edwardian society English lady.

Prezan, Colonel Constantin. Chief of Romanian General Staff, Marshal of Romania.

Pruneau, General. Commander 17th Div at Novisac. French.

Plunkett. British Military Attache at Bucharest.

Queen Marie of Romania (1875–1938). Virtual ruler of Romania.

Ratier, Admiral. French commander of Northern Adriatic.

Renner, Karl. (1870–1950). Austrian Secretary of State of new Republic of Austria.

Sarrail, General Maurice. 1916–Dec. 1917 Supreme Commander Armee Allies en Orient. This was the international force created in 1916 to fight the Ottomans in Bulgaria and Greece. It included French, British, Serbian, Greek and Italian sections.

Schoenborn, Countess Agnes. Cousin and lady in waiting to Empress Zita.

von Seedak, Lt Shonta. Naval officer in charge of communications at Eckartsau.

Strutt, Lt Colonel Edward Lisle Strutt, senior liaison officer between General Milne, commander of the British Macedonian Front and General Henrys, commander of the French Macedonian Army (*Armée d'Orient*).

Szecheny. Countess Yella. A great intriguer and gossip. Knows everyone.

Troubridge, Admiral. (1862–1926). Commander of the Danube and its confluents. Career blighted by not taking on two German warships, SMS *Goeben* and SMS *Breslau* earlier in the war.

Tranier, General. Commander French troops at Zagreb.

Vadrot, Capitaine. General Henry's right hand and fixer.

Windisch Gratz, Princess Otto. (1883–1963). Daughter of Crown Prince Rudolf von Habsburg and Princess Stephanie of Belgium.

Armée d'Afrique – French troops normally serving in Algeria and Tunisia, but brought in to fight in France and Greece.

Armée d'Orient – French divisions normally serving on the Eastern Front.

Index